NATIVE AMERICAN VOICES

To Xavier,
Thanks for your thoughts and
Words. God bless you!
A fellow Sojourner
Blair Goodhouse-Schlepp

NATIVE
AMERICAN
VOICES

▲▼▲▼▲▼▲▼▲

David A. Rausch
& Blair Schlepp

Baker Books

A Division of Baker Book House Co
Grand Rapids, Michigan 49516

© 1994 by David A. Rausch and Blair Schlepp

Published by Baker Books
a division of Baker Book House Company
P.O. Box 6287, Grand Rapids, Michigan 49516-6287

Printed in the United States of America

Library of Congress Cataloging-in-Publication Data

Rausch, David A.
　　Native American voices / David A. Rausch & Blair Schlepp.
　　　　p.　　cm.
　　Includes bibliographical references and index.
　　ISBN 0-8010-7773-7
　　1. Indians of North America—History.　2. Indians of North America—
　Social life and customs.　I. Schlepp, Blair.　II. Title.
　E77.R24　1993　　　　　　　　　　　　　　　　93-45564

To Our Mothers
MARION JUNE PALETTE RAUSCH
LYDIA GOODHOUSE SCHLEPP

She lived in poverty, and yet, she was the richest lady in
the world.
She could not afford a doctor, and yet, she had the world's
Greatest Physician.
She had compassion for the needy, and yet, she respected
and never had an unkind word for those who had plenty.
All of this is true . . . I know . . . because she was my
Mother.

CONTENTS

Introduction   9

1   Native American Groups   21

2   Life before the Conquerors   35

3   The History of Pain   55

4   Regrouping: A Period of Transition   87

5   Religious Encounters   113

6   The Dynamic Community: Problems and
     Prospects   141

Selected Bibliography   165

Index   175

INTRODUCTION

native American Voices takes readers on a historical journey that is on the one hand painful, but on the other hand a celebration of the tenacity and dynamism of the Native American people. It is perhaps fitting that a historian from German, British, French and Scots-Irish heritage (with Johannes Gutenberg as a distant relative on his mother's side), and a counselor from the Lakota Hunkpapa (Sioux) heritage (with Sitting Bull as a distant relative on his mother's side) should collaborate on this book about the Native American experience. David Rausch's distant German relative, Johannes Gutenberg, invented the type mold that made printing from movable metallic type practical. The Mazarin Bible (commonly called the Gutenberg Bible) was the first major endeavor using this typographical method. And yet because of local political squabbles, Gutenberg spent a number of years in exile. Johannes Gutenberg died penniless, but his Bibles are worth a small fortune today.

Blair Schlepp's distant Sioux relative, Sitting Bull, was a respected Native American leader and holy man who spent much time in spiritual pursuits and imparting wisdom to his people. As will be seen in a later chapter, he was forced to flee to Canada in exile, but spent his latter days on the Standing Rock Reservation, a virtual prisoner of the U.S. government until he was murdered. Blair grew up in the same area and is an enrolled member of the Standing Rock Sioux Tribal Reservation. The territory that the U.S. Government and others stole from his people is priceless today.

While a readable historical overview is needed, we have come to this study from the shared viewpoint that this work must also impart the cultural contributions and current status of Native Americans. The dynamism and complexity of this people should be felt as well as the problems and prospects that realistically must be faced in the future. Thus this text may be used in training situations and classrooms as well as being relevant to professionals and interested readers. The plight of Native Americans and the historical atrocities committed against them is currently being unveiled in the media, particularly in film. The success of the movie "Dances with Wolves" and the sensitivity garnered from such an account has underscored the lack of knowledge (and the craving for more information) about the "Indians."

More information on the historical actions of the U.S. government to ignore or overturn treaties, to destroy Native American culture, and to assimilate the tribes into extinction is coming to light daily as 700 Native American lawyers are using the judicial system to right centuries of such abuse and neglect. A coalition of over 35 religious and civil liberties organizations, including the National Association of Evangelicals, the National Council of Churches, and the Union of American Hebrew Congregations came together in the early 1990s to support the "Religious Freedom Restoration Act," a bill seeking to correct the damage done by a Supreme Court ruling on April 17, 1990, against the Native American Church. This book is not only timely, but will add to and integrate publication efforts of the past. The complete Index will help the reader to find information quickly, and a

Selected Bibliography will guide the reader into further specialized study.

Native Americans are a close-knit family, often not divulging information to outsiders. Working together we acquired an inside track to current information and attitudes. We thank the scores of individuals who have shared their deepest perceptions with us. Frankly, the uninitiated individual would be amazed at the different vocations and far-reaching effects of the Native American population. We were impressed anew not only with the fullblooded community, but also with the percentage of the American population that prides itself in having relatives who were Native American. From the Alabama mother of a Greek Orthodox priest, whose Cherokee great grandmother had passed down a heartrending oral tradition concerning the painful march on the "Trail of Tears," to the university chairman of a criminal justice and social welfare department from distant Yankton Sioux tribal background, the heritage was respected. The criminal justice professor remembered the discrimination built into the criminal justice system in the northern plains states in the 1970s, the callousness of some of the judges and law enforcement officials, and the difficulty in being empathetic to Native Americans while keeping one's credibility with officials who ran the system.

In fact, there are many professors and teachers who have distant Native American backgrounds, and their heritage seems to enhance their sensitivity toward dispossessed peoples, their probing analysis of society, and their advocacy of social reform. A good example is the University of Chicago Ph.D, Dr. John C. Cooper, who actually set up the vibrant philosophy program at Eastern Kentucky University in the latter 1960s and has taught at a number of universities and colleges since (only to return to Eastern Kentucky in recent years). A decorated Korean War veteran, John Cooper has written more than 30 books and lectured throughout the world. His paternal great grandfather was of the Blackfoot tribe that was slaughtered by troops, the remnants of the tribe fleeing to Canada. Later some traveled to Oklahoma, linking up with the Five Civilized Nations that were forced to migrate there from the east. Dr. Cooper's grandmother, Anna Jeffers, was reared in a Presbyterian Indian orphanage, and John's father, Chauncey Miller Rose Cooper, never forgot his Native American heritage. When he enlisted in the United States Marine Corp after the First World War, Chauncey Cooper was put in an all-Indian company. For Dr. John C. Cooper, professor of philosophy and religion, his Native American heritage enhances every book he writes and every course he teaches.

Another academician, Dr. Edwin ("Strong-Legs") Richardson, a Penobscot of the Abenaki Confederacy, earned his Ph.D. in health and social rehabilitation administration from Ohio State University in 1951. Former Chief of Behavorial Sciences in the Department of International Studies at the U.S. military's Green Beret School, he has the distinction of being the first Native American psychologist in the United States. He developed a culturalization test for the Lakota Sioux that was bilingual and, in some cases, a much better projective test than those designed for whites (such as the MMPI). Dr. Richardson has worked in various departments of the federal government to solve Native American problems, and has been highly acclaimed for his research and writing. He has also dedicated his life to nurturing Native American students (as well as other students) to follow in his footsteps.

Dr. Don Bartlette is one example of the thousands of Native Americans who have grown up in debilitating social and physical circumstances and have risen to overcome the overwhelming obstacles. Born with a cleft palate and harelip into a dysfunctional Chippewa family that was racked by alcoholism and abuse, young Don seemed destined for a life of delinquency and misery. Rejected by his father, he was befriended by a kindly woman who saw potential in him and raised him as her own. She spent countless hours patiently teaching him to speak and gave him the nurturing and love to help him conquer his emotional, social and physical scars. He eventually attended college and graduate school, receiving his Ph.D. in Speech Pathology. Incredibly, he became a nationally known public speaker and the first social worker to be accepted into the American Academy on Mental Retardation. He and his wife have raised eight of their own children and have provided a foster home for a number of others with special needs. Dr. Don Bartlette has dedicated his life to helping the physically handicapped, and in his autobiographical profile "Macaroni at Midnight," he has spoken to thousands of groups across the United States of his own experiences growing up as a Chippewa child.

Scars run deep in the Native American community, and in spite of the intense pride and resilience of some, those scars have not healed evenly. We were overwhelmed, however, as we came across evidence of intense prejudice and hatred toward Native American brothers and sisters that still infest some white families. For example, on the Mescalero Reservation in southcentral New Mexico, Ouida Miller, a granddaughter of the famed Chiricahua Apache Geronimo, still receives hate mail from men and women in Arizona, descendants of those killed by her grandfather. Nearing her seventies, Ouida treasures her knowledge of her grandfather's history and a more complete account of his reasons for rebellion, flight, and fight. But it is difficult to persuade those white families that have harbored their hatred for over a century, and they seem to be blind to the devastation inflicted upon Native Americans. Lakota tribal member Johnson Holy Rock explains this phenomenon as he speaks with visitors from around the United States: "The indian was in the way of what the whites term as 'progress.' We were an obstacle to the progress of the nation, and because we were an obstacle, we had to be removed."

In many parts of the country there are Native Americans who have dedicated their remaining days on earth to preserving what remains of their heritage and culture. Stanley Bahnimtewa, who is Hopi chief of Old Oraibi in Arizona, the oldest continuously inhabited village in the United States (settled 400 years before Columbus), insists that he will fight against electricity and electric lines infesting his ancient village "as long as I'm leader." He sputters about modernization and the toll it has taken on Native American culture.

Across the country in Montville, Connecticut, Gladys Tantaquidgeon labors lovingly in her family's "Indian Museum." In her nineties, she is one of the last of the nearly fullblooded Mohegans, the Wolf Clan, an offshoot of the Mohicans portrayed in the 1992 Twentieth Century Fox movie, "The Last of the Mohicans." Gladys' father John and his brother Harold built the museum in 1931 to store all of the Native American photographs and artifacts they had collected. Now Gladys has inspired her nieces to learn more of their Mohegan heritage and to take interest in the Indian Museum.

As a girl Gladys was chosen by the older women of the tribe to learn their ancient knowledge about folk medicine and to steep herself in tribal folklore. As a young woman Gladys studied anthropology at the University of Pennsylvania, working for over a decade in the west with the tribes of the Great Plains. Never married, she came back to southern New England. To Gladys Tantaquidgeon, the museum is her "child." She patiently teaches over one thousand visitors a year how the early natives lived and what traditions they held dear. She is convinced that the early European settlers in southern New England would not have survived without help from the Mohegans. Her family and many tribal members were converted to Christianity and tried to work hand in hand with the European settlers. Today, Gladys is laboring to reconstruct the Mohegan language, a language that had been forsaken over a century ago because of the opposition of those from European backgrounds. Like so many of the dedicated Native Americans we have encountered in many parts of this land, she works long hours to heal the pain of her people and to preserve their rich heritage.

Another impressive group of Native Americans is that working within the political labyrinth of the United States government. While radical political activists receive quite a bit of news coverage from time to time, there is also a group of Native Americans working quietly and efficiently to better the condition of their people. And, as they better conditions for their own people, they benefit the American people as a whole. One such individual is Ron Andrade, a member of the La Jolla tribe in San Diego and of Luiseno and Diegueno Native American background. As a Californian of Native American heritage Ron has dedicated his life to promoting the interests of his people in Washington, D.C.

A graduate of the urban studies program at Antioch University in Los Angeles, Ron was elected vice-chairman of the Inter-Tribal Council of California before the age of thirty. By the age of thirty-three he was appointed executive director of the National Congress of American Indians (NCAI), the oldest and largest Native American organization in the United States. Representing 180 tribal governments and over 350,000 Native Americans in Washington, D.C., Ron Andrade was responsible for all legislative and research activities sponsored by NCAI, including briefings for Congress and the White House.

In 1983 he became staff assistant to the Assistant Secretary for Indian Affairs in the U.S. Department of Interior, and from 1984–1986 worked in a similar capacity for the Director of the Office of Civil Rights in the U.S. Department of Agriculture. This was the first time such a position had been created at the departmental level in the Department of Agriculture, and Ron was responsible for reviewing and critiquing regulations that impacted on the Native American community. With this wealth of experience he was appointed by President Bush to the National Advisory Council on Indian Education within the U.S. Department of Education, again maintaining responsibility for legislation, regulations, and grant proposals. In each position Ron Andrade worked diligently to ascertain the condition of Native American communities across the United States and to help them, while he and his wife raised seven children to respect their Native American heritage. Few of his friends know the extent of his efforts over the past two decades, or of his new responsibilities concerning education, technology, and business development on behalf of Native American communities. He quietly and humbly labors on.

In the Congress itself, Democrat Ben Nighthorse Campbell from Colorado is much more noticeable these days. The first chief to serve in the U.S. House of Representatives (three terms), Ben was elected to a Senate seat in 1992, the first Native American to serve in that capacity since 1929 (Kansas bred Charles Curtis was the Native American senator who gave up his post to serve as Herbert Hoover's vice president). Great-grandson of Black Horse, a Cheyenne who fought at the Little Big Horn, Ben Nighthorse Campbell overcame a traumatic childhood of orphanages and foster homes to earn his degree in education at San Jose State University in the 1950s.

By 1960 Ben Nighthorse Campbell was studying judo in Tokyo, Japan, and in 1963 won a gold medal at the Pan Am Games. In 1964 Ben captained the U.S. Olympic judo team, coming in fourth overall, and in a moving experience carried the U.S. flag in the closing ceremonies. The 1964 Tokyo Olympic Games were the very same Olympics in which Native American Billy Mills, a 26-year-old Marine lieutenant from Pine Ridge, South Dakota, captured the gold medal in the 10,000 meter race. Together, the Lakota Mills and the Northern Cheyenne Campbell join a group of at least a dozen Native American Olympic champions, including the legendary Jim Thorpe from the Sac and Fox-Potawatomi tribe.

Today, Ben Nighthorse Campbell is known as much for his jewelry-making skills as he is for his political career (a career that began in 1982 when he walked into a political meeting to support a friend and was drafted for political office himself). He has garnered over 200 awards for jewelry design and highly values his artistry. A political maverick and self-styled moderate who votes his conscience and sides with Republicans as much as with Democrats, Ben Nighthorse Campbell refuses to operate within party politics. "I'll take the heat," he insists. On the national scene he attempts to build a bridge between the Native American community, the white community, and other minority groups. He quietly maintains, "You can't keep hate alive."

Such are but a few of the famed individuals we have encountered in our pursuit of *Native American Voices*. It must be remembered, however, that while the above examples underscore the different vocations and far-reaching effects of the Native American population in the United States today, there are hundreds of thousands of "average" Native Americans who bravely carry on in their daily duties and with their family obligations. These mothers and fathers, grandmothers and grandfathers, rarely receive fanfare or applause, but are the role models that most greatly impact a new generation of Native Americans. The variety of individuals that we have discussed here does show, nevertheless, that in an American culture that requires national role models, Native Americans have an abundant share as well.

Native American Voices is dedicated to our mothers, who have left us a heritage of understanding and compassion. David Rausch's mother, June, is in active retirement, beloved by her many friends and a constant encouragement to her children and grandchildren. Blair's mother, Mrs. Lydia Goodhouse Schlepp, was a good example of the hundreds of thousands of Native American mothers who have dedicated their lives to their children and their communities. The second oldest child of Moses and Clementine Goodhouse, Lydia was raised in a large Native American household that encouraged religion and family as important aspects in the preservation of family and culture. She became a Christian in 1966 and returned to her reservation to testify to her new relationship with God. She even went back to college for a religious education to help in this endeavor. At her funeral in 1986 her brother-in-law challenged those in attendance: "Here lies a sister that loved us, she came back and spoke to us, sang to us, and prayed for us. Now which of you is going to take her place? Which of you will return to us and live among us? She left a legacy for her children to follow."

In 1993 a Native American comedian entertained a packed audience and switched to the subject of his heritage and his people. He informed the giggling crowd, who were impressed with his wit and charm, that the Europeans came to America and declared "we discovered it!" without any mention of those who were already here. As the audience listened attentively, he proceeded: "Then the Europeans declared that the land was theirs because the Native Americans were 'not using it.'" The Native American comedian insisted that it was time his people used the same logic. "I noticed a beautiful red Ferrari in the studio parking lot," he told the audience, and then pretending to steer a wheel and shaking his long black hair as though it were blowing in the breeze, he dogmatically stated: "I now claim that sports car because the owner is *not using* his Ferrari!"

Although the audience laughed hysterically at his antics, there was a bitter historical truth to what the Native American comedian was alluding. Our journey in *Native American Voices* begins with an overview of the various regions of what became the United States and the variety of tribal groups that settled there. We then consider what Native American life was like before the European conquerors and the subsequent history of pain. Chapters exploring governmental and religious encounters follow in an effort to broaden and update the reader's knowledge of this diverse people. With every chapter we build another layer of perception on this complicated tale. We conclude in chapter six with the dynamic community itself, exploring the unique psyche of the Native American, contributions and assets as well as problems and prospects. May your journey into this fascinating world and intriguing history be sobering as well as enlightening.

David A. Rausch   Blair Schlepp
Ashland, Ohio   Reston, Virginia

1

NATIVE AMERICAN GROUPS

A man from a diverse European heritage was visibly incensed. He had written a letter to the editor angrily denouncing Native American protests in the last decade of the twentieth century. He was fed up with "all" protests, and his bold statements had won him, a self-styled "average American," national attention. "I feel this protesting is ridiculous," he declared, "it is five hundred years since Columbus came into this country. . . ." The Native American educator who sat next to him looked stoically ahead until asked by the commentator, "How do you respond to that?" "I agree with him . . . five hundred years *is* a long time," the Native American answered, turning to the man with sincere piercing eyes, "We realize you are slow learners, but five hundred years is a *real long time.*"

Later, the man who hated protests again in exasperation questioned: "But why have you waited five hundred years to protest." The Native American once again turned to him and said: "We've tried to, but you've never listened. . . ."

American historians have often given great emphasis to the westward movement, glorifying Europeans and other immigrants who for the past four hundred years have moved across the vast stretch of land that separates the Atlantic from

the Pacific. In fact, courses entitled "The Westward Movement" are included in most university history curriculums.
To the average citizen of the United States this movement
into the "frontier" was part and parcel of the inception of this
great land.

Ironically, in contrast to the few centuries in which the
European "westward movement" expanded, it was preceded
by an eastward and southward "frontier movement," a mass
migration of peoples that had been occurring for millennia!
This was the frontier movement of the Native Americans,
men and women who with their families migrated across a
temporary land bridge between the barren land of Siberia and
the area of present-day Alaska. For thousands of years these
peoples of Asian Mongoloid stock spread south and east in
search of food and a better life, soon developing distinct cultures across territories that today encompass the arctic regions,
Canada, the United States (west, north, south, and east),
Central America, and South America (to its southernmost
reaches). Thus it was a very "old" world that European explorers and their benefactors called the New World.

The European explorers lumped these diverse and complex cultures of Native Americans into the simplistic cate-
gory, Indian. European settlers continued the stereotype.
These "Indians" were believed to be heathen savages. All
"Indians" were considered to be "the same." Little did European settlers realize that more than two thousand languages
were spoken by the indigenous Native American tribal
groups, languages more distinct than English is from French.
Furthermore, the Native American cultures that existed on
the American continent when Europeans first reached the
"New World" differed greatly from one another. They were
in different cultural stages, lived in strikingly different homes,
and sought their livelihood in varied fashions. In many ways,

it was the Europeans who were "much the same" when contrasted to the wide range of Native American life.

Anthropologists have separated this North American migration into as many as twelve culture areas, regions both distinct and diverse in their composition due to climate and resources. Concentrating mainly on the territory that became "the lower 48" of the United States, we have decided to analyze four regions (which we refer to as Southwest, Eastern Woodlands, Prairie-Plains, and West-Northwest), understanding the fact that there are tribes of Native Americans that occupied the frigid territories of the arctic and subarctic as well as tribes that occupied the far warmer Mexican territory and Mesoamerica. Each of these tribes has a distinguished and ancient history of its own; it is hoped that our initial study will provoke the reader to learn more of the rich heritage of all of these groups. For our purposes, however, it is important to refer to sample cultural regions to underscore the diversity and ingenuity of tribal groups that settled in each.

▼ Southwest

The Southwest region includes the modern states of Arizona and New Mexico, expanding in three directions into southern Colorado, southern Utah, southeastern California, and northern Mexico. Diverse Native American cultural traditions developed in this area. Hunting and gathering gave way to a more sedentary planting of crops. A group of Native Americans migrating from Mexico into southern Arizona c. 300 B.C. established a town on the plain along the Gila River, planting in the flood deposits and building irrigation channels for better water distribution. The Pima and Papago peoples descended from these early settlers, living on small farms (*rancherias*), some to the present day. To their west in a sector that bordered California, the Yuma peoples cultivated crops along the Colorado River and its tributaries. They did not build towns but worked individual *rancherias*. The Yuma peoples thus did not attract the attention of the Spanish explorers and armies who were interested in more substantial colonies.

To the north, tribes that built homes in dry caves or rock shelters before the time of Christ began constructing villages of round homes. Developing more oval shaping to their substantial shelters, they soon were living in rectangular structures by 700 A.D., and were cultivating a new variety of high-yield flour maize. This culture became the "Pueblo" culture characterized by the Hopi and Zuni peoples. At first these rectangular homes were built in pits with attached anterooms, but with the development of stone masonry, multistory pueblos with hundreds of rooms blossomed. From 1100–1300 A.D. planned villages of these large terraced apartments could house over a thousand people each. The multistory, multifamily pueblos were built around open public areas. Pueblo society learned to bring precious water to its sunbaked habitat by employing irrigation canals, terracing, and damming techniques to increase crop production. And yet such Native American societies have their own distictions. Among the Pueblo peoples of the Southwest at least six different languages were spoken from four different language stocks.

The ancestors of the Apache and Navajo appear to be the "newcomers" in the Native American Southwest. Approximately one hundred years before the Spanish arrived, nomadic bison hunters with limited agricultural experience, moving in groups of a few families, raided pueblos. Speaking the Athabascan language, these ancestors of the Apaches and Navajos seem to have originated in Canada, traveling south along the plains into Colorado. Some groups took over pueblos that had been abandoned and added agricultural specialization to their society, while other groups remained bison-oriented. The Navajos and the Western Apache are representative of the former, the Eastern Apache of the latter. Today the Navajo number nearly 200,000 members and hold approximately 16 million acres of reservation land (25,000 square miles). This makes them the largest single Native American tribe in the United States.

▼ Eastern Woodlands

To the east, Native American "mound builders" were constructing edifices along the Ohio and Mississippi rivers that would puzzle European explorers centuries later. This Hopewell Period (c. 300 B.C. to 600 A.D.) flourished during the time of the birth of Christ, leaving a legacy of mounds and gigantic sculptured earthworks in the shapes of serpents, birds, humans, and other ceremonial designs. In the Ohio Valley, ten thousand of these earthen heaps dotted the landscape. One near Miamisburg, Ohio was nearly 70 feet high and 850 feet in circumference. It was estimated to contain over 300,000 cubic feet of soil.

The leaders of the Hopewell civilization organized thousands of Native American villages and farms into a network for trade and service. Districts were subject to the will of this elite from the Great Lakes to the Gulf of Mexico. Some of the mounds appear to be grand burial edifices, while the shapes of others seem to signify mysterious ceremonial and religious rituals. So impressive were the numbers, sizes, and shapes of these mounds, and so demeaning was the European view of the natives who occupied the land, that later European settlers theorized that an ancient race of gifted artisans had traveled from the "Old World" to the "New World" to construct them. Legends concerning the lost civilization of Atlantis, or ancient Hebrews, Egyptians, Phoenicians, Hindus, or Vikings took root, only to be dispelled by later archeological excavation.

The Hopewell culture diminished and was soon replaced by another Native American culture, the Mississippian, around 750 A.D. Named for its origin in the Mississippi Valley and Gulf Coast, this culture was noted for its intensive cultivation of maize, beans, and squash, as well as new towns that dotted fertile farmland. Around 950 A.D. the Native American city of Cahokia was laid out near present-day East St. Louis. By 1100 A.D. Cahokia covered six square miles and had an estimated population of 40,000. Serving as the commercial center and urban metropolis of Mississipian culture, Cahokia was surrounded by more than 120 ceremonial mounds. At the center of the city stood a massive mound covering 15 acres and headed by a large plaza. Built over the span of two centuries, this mound was 100 feet high and contained 22 million cubic feet of clay, silt, and sand. The archeological artifacts recovered from Cahokia and her gravesites point to a stratified urban society that could boast proficiency in fine craftsmanship and near-modern specialization of tasks. Trade was conducted in a large territory from Lake Superior to the Atlantic Ocean, from Texas to Wisconsin.

Although in serious decline by the time the Europeans explored the area, the Hopewell and Mississipian cultures had spread eastward, influencing woodland societies in the southeast and northeast.

Southeast Woodlands

The tribes of the Southeast had been part of the Hopewell network, and Creeks, Choctaws, and Natchez (among others) could claim the Mound Builders as their ancestors. Mississipian culture furthered such motifs. European explorers of the Southeast found towns with plazas and mounds, and described customs that emulated Cahokian society. Although many of the languages spoken by Native Americans in the Southeast are now extinct, they appear to be from at least five language families: Algonkian, Caddoan, Iroquoian, Musko-gean, and Siouan. These families give clues as to the migra-tion patterns of the respective tribes. Diversity is evident in that each of these language families can be broken into a vari-ety of language groups. For example, the Muskogean language family includes Alabama-Koasati, Apalachee, Choctaw-Chickasaw, Mikasuki-Hitchiti, and Muskogee-Seminole. The Muskogean language family even provided place names in Alabama (including Tuscaloosa, Tuskegee, and Talladega), and river names in Alabama and Georgia (including Chat-tahoochee, Ocmulgee, and Tallapoosa). Even the word "Alabama" is from the Muskogean language family. In like manner, the Iroquoian language family includes Cherokee, which in turn provided such designations as "Tennessee."

The Native American Southeast culture area encompassed the coastal plain that stretched from eastern Texas through Louisiana, Alabama, Florida, Georgia, North and South Car-olina, and into the coastal area of Virginia. The highlands of Arkansas, Missouri, and southern Appalachia (incorporating parts of Kentucky, Tennessee, West Virginia, and Virginia) and the areas at the base of the eastern mountains (called the Piedmont) formed the interior western and northern boundaries. Three-quarters of the Southeast culture area was coastal plain and had a rich variety of mammals, birds, fruits, vegetables, and trees. Native Americans keenly adapted their lifestyles and customs to the environmental conditions of their respective habitats. One is impressed as well with their elaborate ceramic and weaving techniques, and their ability to conduct long-distance trade.

Northeast Woodlands

In the Northeast, a steady population growth of Native American hunters and fishermen thousands of years before

Christ parallels the time period of the pyramid-building Egyptian dynasties in the Ancient Near East. From c. 300 B.C. well into the first millennium A.D., there is ample evidence of small nomadic Native American communities that built rectangular houses and buried their dead with tools, antler combs, and jewelry for the next world. Only around 1000 A.D. is there evidence of an agricultural revolution, focusing on the domestication of maize, sunflowers, beans, and squash. Trade in furs and meat increased. The Algonkian language family predominated the coast north to south, from Canada through Maine, New Hampshire, Connecticut, and down to Virginia; while the Iroquoian language family formed a solid pattern from the eastern Great Lakes through upstate New York. The Algonkians depended more on hunting and gathering, the Iroquoians depended more on cultivation (although both groups engaged in each according to climatic conditions).

Infighting and tribal animosities escalated in the 1400s. With European contact, Algonkian tribes and Iroquoian tribes began vying for trade. Ancient enmities led to ceaseless warfare between the coastal Algonkians and the inland Iroquoians during the fifteenth and sixteenth centuries. The territory surrounding the Gulf of St. Lawrence turned into a bloody battleground. Villages in this area were abandoned and polarization increased. It was the legendary Mohawk, Hiawatha, who convinced village after village, tribe after tribe, to unite together into what Europeans called The League of Five Nations of the Iroquois. Overwhelmed by grief over the murder of his family, Hiawatha had fled into the forests, living as a hermit until he met Dekanawida, a Huron visionary who believed that the tribes could be freed from warfare and devastation by allying themselves in a great league. Slow of speech, Dekanawida needed the imposing and articulate Hiawatha to convey the message across the North-east.

Together Dekanawida and Hiawatha traveled long distances throughout the Northeast, and together they convinced five tribes to unite into *Ganonsyoni* ("The Lodge Extended Lengthwise"). The five nations incorporated as such were the Cayugas ("People at the Landing"), the Mohawks ("People of Flint"), the Oneidas ("People of the Stone"), the Onondagas ("People of the Mountain"), and the Senecas ("Great Hill People"). Imbued with the Eastern Woodland's traditions, this Iroquois confederation encompassed as many as ten thousand Native Americans by 1600. Ironically, Dekanawida's Huron people did not join the league and were considered enemies on the outside (as were other "outside" tribes such as the Erie and Susquehannock). While peace was elusive, the Iroquois Confederacy protected extensive fertile lands from enemy tribal raids and amassed a power in military and trade that was unprecedented in the Northeast. Early in the eighteenth century the Iroquois Confederacy would become Six Nations when a Southeast people, the Tuscarora refugees from North Carolina, joined the confederation.

▼ Prairie-Plains

Prairies begin in the area of the Canadian province of Saskatchewan and dominate the landscape from North and South Dakota (brushing the southwestern corner of Minnesota and the northwestern corner of Iowa), through Nebraska, Kansas, and Oklahoma, into Texas. The High Plains begin in the area of the Canadian province of Alberta, and dominate the landscape from Montana, through eastern Wyoming, eastern Colorado, and a portion of eastern New Mexico, into Texas. Regions that we have already studied had a great influence on this Prairie-Plains region. Tribes from the

Eastern Woodland region began to influence the Prairie-
Plains region around 500 B.C., continuing periodic interac-
tions and migrations well into the first millennia A.D. Near
the time of Christ, trade with the Hopewell Culture of the
Southeast appears to have influenced a movement toward villages in the Prairie-Plains region.

We have noted how the Apaches from Canada moved
through the region. Some scholars theorize that the first true
arrow points on the Prairie-Plains were due to this movement.
Migrations continued to occur. During the 1400s, for example, the Blackfoot tribes were firmly established on the plains,
while some of the Apache tribes were entrenched in Colorado. It appears that the Shoshoni peoples entered Wyoming
during the same century. The Prairie-Plains region, however,
was not dominated by nomadic peoples. Since the mid-800s,
Native American villages of rectangular homes and cultivated fields dotted the Prairie-Plains region as far north as the
South Dakota area. Although these Plains' farmers engaged
in extensive bison hunts, their family and village life was stable. By 1450 A.D. villages of farmer-hunters were composed
of as many as one hundred homes. Tribes throughout the
region vacillated between a predilection for settlement and
a predilection for nomadic hunting and gathering. Often climatic conditions dictated a necessary choice.

Nevertheless, the foundation of the Prairie-Plains culture
was the bison, affecting Native American life from the prairies
west of the Mississipi Valley to the Rocky Mountains. Bands
of fifty to one hundred persons were foundational to the
Prairie-Plains region, because this number of individuals could
handle a bison drive. Annual controlled burning of the grasslands produced especially tender shoots of new grass. These,
in turn, attracted many herds of bison to the same area in the
early summer. The bison were driven into a corral, sometimes
using the stone structures of a ravine or bluff and adding a

fence made out of poles and brush. Bows and arrows revolutionized the hunt around 500 A.D., while the arrival of European horses from the Southwest in the 1700s changed the lifestyle of the Native Americans as drastically as the automobile would change the American people in the twentieth century. Whole tribes began to live on horseback, dragging mobile *tipis* behind. Narrow European concepts about Native Americans were prejudiced by viewing such movements.

The Sioux and their eagle-feather headdresses have symbolized Native Americans throughout the world. And yet, even the Sioux are much more complex than the popular "Wild West" concepts would allow. For example, at least seven divisions of Sioux, each with its subdivisions, occupied the land when the Europeans arrived. There were four eastern Santee Dakota divisions (Mdewakanton, Sisseton, Wahpekute, and Wahpeton), two "middle" territory Nakota divisions (Yankton and Yanktonai), and the western division, the Lakota or Teton. In the 1600s this variety of Sioux tribes occupied most of Minnesota, flanked by the Cheyenne to the south and the Chippewa in Wisconsin. The Santee Sioux in northeastern Minnesota relied on deer as well as bison, and spent considerable time in agricultural pursuits. The Teton Sioux of western Minnesota were the prairie people for whom bison were extremely important. The Nakota tribes (Yankton and Yanktonai) had gardens and fished, but were close to the prairies for bison hunting. In the early 1700s, as the fur trade was established around the Great Lakes and Mississippi, the Lakota and Nakota shifted westward into North and South Dakota. In the broad territory that separated the Eastern Woodlands region from the High Plains, Yanktonai served as middlemen in trade between the Tetons and Santee.

As will be seen in chapters three and four, the treachery of United States government officials, the greed and prejudice of settlers from European roots, the needless liquidation of the bison population, and the forced removal of eastern tribes would complicate the history of Native Americans in the Prairie-Plains region.

▼ West-Northwest

According to many experts, the most linguistically diverse area in North America was the California-Oregon and Northwest coast area of the United States. California alone had over five hundred tribes and a number of culture areas. Along the Pacific coast, Native Americans specialized in fishing, and the coastal tribes of northern California, Oregon, and Washington were noted for their large canoes and plank houses. Centuries before Christ, heavy woodworking tools were developed to split tall cedars, redwoods, and fir trees. By 500 A.D. patterns of fishing and building were firmly entrenched. These Native Americans were highly conscious of social standing, arranging marriages among their aristocracy with those of noble birth in other tribes. Chiefs were carefully chosen from this nobility, depending on specially trained spiritual "doctors" to remove disease and thwart enemies.

Native Americans along the Pacific had abundant and dependable sources of food, including fish, seals, sea lions, otters, and whales. Groups of salmon fishermen, such as the Yurok of northern California, had five species of Pacific salmon from which to choose. In addition to fishing and the hunting of fur seals, the Makah on the tip of the Washington coast, between the ocean and the forest, made whaling a regular pursuit. In fact, the Makah word for "fish" is the same word the tribe used for "food." They excelled in woodworking, as did many of the tribes of northern California and the Northwest.

Both the Yurok of California and the Makah of Washington spoke languages belonging to the Algonkian language family. This language family spread to many parts of America, including the Northeast. In fact, the first European linguistic breakthrough was by a missionary, John Eliot, who in 1663 translated the Bible into Massachusett, an Algonkian language (see chapter five). He later published an Algonkian grammar in 1666. While Native American customs could be disdained or ignored by European settlers, Native American languages could not be ignored if one wished to communicate or convert. Certainly the language development of Native Americans was as diverse and complicated as their cultural development. Language can provide a key to understanding native culture, and understanding certain aspects of a tribe's language often helps one to discern the dimensions of human life and lifestyle. That European settlers in most cases ignored Native American languages as well as Native American cultures is a sad commentary on a subsequent history of prejudice and misunderstanding.

President Thomas Jefferson was one of the first prominent collectors of information on Native American linguistics. Jefferson believed that it was possible to trace the relationships among tribes through language association, and two hundred years ago he worried that these languages would disappear before such associations could be determined. As President, Thomas Jefferson commissioned the Lewis and Clark Expedition (1804–1806). His written instructions to Captain Meriwether Lewis in 1803 stated in part,

> In all your intercourse with the natives treat them in the most friendly & conciliatory manner which their own conduct will admit; allay all jealousies as to the object of your journey, satisfy them of it's innocence, make them acquainted with the position, extent, character, peaceable & commercial dispositions of the U.S. of our wish to be neighborly, friendly & useful to them, & of our dispositions to a commercial inter-

course with them; confer with them on the points most con-venient as mutual emporiums, & the articles of most desire-able interchange for them & us.

Little could President Jefferson envision the blows that would be inflicted during the nineteenth century on Native American life.

2

LIFE BEFORE THE CONQUERORS

During the summer of 1992, Tom Warren and John Hilton traveled the route that the Lewis and Clark Expedition had traveled nearly two hundred years before. For Warren, this was the fulfillment of a lifelong dream. As a nine-year-old he had read a book on Lewis and Clark, envisioning that some day he too would make the same journey. Now with high-tech gear, two years of careful planning for any obstacles, and a summer free, he and his colleague from Middlebury College left St. Louis for Oregon country. When interviewed in August, near the end of their journey, Tom Warren noted that he was "scared" by the condition of the nation's rivers and the environmental disaster that surrounded them. Both men thought they "knew" about such environmental problems, but they were unprepared for the ecological disasters they encountered. Referring to the contrast between the Lewis and Clark Expedition journals and the reality they faced, Warren shook his head: "Lewis and Clark wrote about pristine rivers."

Indeed, Lewis and Clark's journals are filled with descriptions of beautiful landscapes, an abundance of game, and a clean environment. For example, on July 22, 1805, Captain Meriwether Lewis described in his own hand (and with his own spelling and punctuation) a pristine river on which he had hunted. "I kiled an otter which sunk to the bottom on being shot, a circumstance unusual with that anamal. *the water was about 8 feet deep yet so clear that I could see it at the bottom*; I swam in and obtained it by diving. I halted the party here for dinner."

Today, two centuries later, nonpolluted water, soil, and air can no longer be taken for granted. We have lost the intimate connection with the land that typified Native American culture before the European conquest. We have "muddied the waters" in less than two hundred years; an environment Native Americans had cherished and protected for more than two thousand years. In this chapter we will view in part general Native American lifestyles and customs endemic to the regions discussed in chapter one. We will catch a glimpse of Native American life before the conquerors.

▼ The Pueblos of the Southwest

The Western Pueblo culture exhibited by the Hopis and Zunis is intimately connected with their desert landscape. Here, past and present blend in a continuous Southwestern lifestyle. Farming this arid expanse of unpredictable rainfall depended on rainwater seeping from the upward sandstone regions down into moist valley floors and springs. Enduring periodic droughts that sapped their resources (and led many neighbors to abandon settlements), the Hopi and Zuni pueblos lived on subsistence farming of crops, and periodic hunting and gathering. Continuously inhabiting their pueblos centuries before the Spaniards arrived in 1540, the Hopi and Zuni pueblos exhibited an understanding and respect for the environment.

On the eve of European conquest, the Western Pueblos were organized in matrilineal clans, tracing their lineage through mothers and daughters. Women owned the houses and lands, and husbands had to move in with their wives. If divorced, the husbands would have to return to the home of their mothers and sisters. The extended family and traditional ceremony dominated the social unit of the pueblo, and each clan maintained a ceremonial chamber with ritual objects. Consisting of a grandmother, her daughters, the daughters' daughters, the daughters' husbands, and unmarried sons, the extended family nurtured the life of each child born into it. These relatives guided the child in spiritual education and daily tasks necessary to become a productive and responsible member of the clan.

While kinship was the most important element in the social structure of Pueblo society, cross-clan membership in ceremonial societies prevented undue power from residing in one family or group. In contrast to the female dominant role in lineage and home, men played the significant role in the ceremonies. In a precarious natural environment, religious observance pervaded all of Pueblo life, and ritual expression emphasized unity and cooperation. There were ceremonial societies with separate priesthoods, secret rituals, secret holy objects, legends of origin, and separate yearly cycles in dedication to the sun as the source of life, the waters as sustainers of life, ancestors, and mythical heroes. Both corporate and individual ceremonies implored supernatural powers for good health, good harvests, and peaceful coexistence. Every movement, symbol, and chant had meaning, whether in dance, mask, or song. Adolescent boys coming-of-age were initiated into a ceremonial society, the secret rites looked upon as birth into adulthood. Religious rites preceded the planting of a crop or the building of a house. Every facet of nature was honored and respected, and volumes could be written on the intrica-

cies of worship among clans, pueblos, and tribes. To complicate matters, even though Native American Pueblos today
continue many of the same facets of ritual, it is difficult to
completely reconstruct the thoughts and views of the Pueblo
religious practice before the conquerors arrived. The ancient
views surface, however, in current legend and religious practice.

The Zuni pueblos believed that there were the "raw people" and the "cooked people" who inhabited the earth. The
cooked people ate cooked food and were people of the daylight. The raw people ate raw food or food that was sacrificed
to them by the cooked people. Environment was integrally
connected in that even the earth was a person, part of the
raw people. Trees were her arms and flora her covering. The
Sun Father was the giver of light and life, the one who held
the destiny of each person. He created the cooked people out
of the fourth underworld to commune with him through
prayer and offerings. The Sun Father blesses his creation with
daylight and rewards those who are faithful.

The Hopi pueblos believed that there was a reason the Sun
makes his daily journey through the upper world of the living and the lower world of the dead. All existence has inter-
twining relationships. Day and night, life and death, summer
and winter, are not in stark opposition, but rather compose a
total system of one substance or essence. "Death" is actually
"Birth" into a new world, and Hopi burial ceremonies have
many of the same elements as the ceremonies at birth. Even
human beings had a physical body and a spirit or soul, the
"breath body." While there is a duality assigned to time, space,
number, and color, there is an accompanying complex integration of these factors into a complete philosophical system
of life and meaning.

The Native American Pueblos are surrounded with a dazzling landscape of hundreds of shades of orange, yellow, pur-

ple, and red. The blue sky with white clouds and dazzling sun contrast against the rugged mesas and crooked valleys. Little wonder that colors have been used for thousands of years as symbolic classifiers among the Pueblos. Each direction on the horizon, including up and down, has a color or combination of colors assigned to it. Legends use colors to signify hierarchical position and creation order. The spirit world is emphasized with shadowy, contrasting colors.

▼ The Potlatch of the West-Northwest

In some ways, the Native American communities of the Northwest "lower 48" presented quite a contrast to the Pueblo peoples of the Southwest. The most important lineage ties were patrilineal, the male line being dominant (with notable exceptions), although the female lineage could have considerable importance for family ties and rights to hunt and fish. Life prospered in the relatively mild climate. There was an abundant supply of food along the Pacific coast, and the Yurok of northern California and the Makah of Washington were surrounded by bounteous waters and lush forests. Trees were plentiful, and many of the peoples of the Northwest "lower 48" area occupied permanent villages composed of plank houses. Others had both winter and summer homes. Woodworking crafts and tools were well developed, from intricate carvings to heavy equipment. Large dugout canoes traveled the sea, and massive wooden totem poles and giant figures soon dotted the region. To the peoples of the West-Northwest, there was a mystical link between the woods and the water.

Social organization in the West-Northwest put great emphasis on wealth and birth. A "chief" gained power through his lineage and the increasing economic power of his relatives. There were no formal councils to appoint leaders or to tie villages together, but a nobility of rank and privilege headed a stratified Native American society. To strengthen these bonds and accumulate wealth marriages were arranged for young people by noble-born parents of autonomous villages. Claims to chiefly status were validated through a gift-giving feast, the potlatch ("give"), which was an important characteristic of the political, economic, social, and religious life of the region.

Most villages had a large wooden plank house (perhaps 100 feet in length) built for the specific purpose of holding potlatches. Constructed close to a water passage so that guests had easy access, the potlatch house sometimes served as the home of the village leader as well as the center of festive occasions. The potlatch combined ritual and tradition with prestige and honor. It could be held in thanksgiving for a successful fishing expedition, or in lieu of a potential marriage. A potlatch was often held on the occasion of a noble child entering adulthood, or as a memorial for a deceased relative.

It was customary for the chief or a wealthy noble to lead the potlatch, impressing guests from other villages with the prosperity of his family and village. Traditional songs and festivity set the mood for these occasions, and games and sports were combined with more than ample food, magical tricks, and speeches. Some songs were actually "owned" by a tribal family, and singing was extremely important to this culture. Central to the potlatch, however, were the lavish gifts bestowed upon the formally invited guests, accompanied by the leadership claims of those in charge and the subsequent bestowal of honor upon the leaders by those in attendance. To dispute a claim made at a potlatch, leaders in other villages would have to hold a similar or more grandiose potlatch. Within larger villages, a wealthy noble could state his family claims through a potlatch.

Although fish and mammals were abundant in the North-west, the Native Americans in this plush area had rites and restrictions to avoid wasteful management of their environment. They believed that fish and mammals had a spirit as well as a physical body. When a fish or mammal was killed for food it was believed that only the physical form was consumed. The spirit of the salmon or deer continued to exist. Therefore, prayers and ceremonial ritual preceded any hunting or fishing excursion. Male and female spiritual doctors tapped into this spiritual phenomena to heal both physical and psychological diseases. Young people were also taught to respect traditional family values, maintain their chastity until marriage, and uphold the honor of the family by never bringing shame upon it.

A number of the tribes of the West-Northwest viewed the earth on which they stood as a circular island that rested on the waters. The rise and fall of the land was caused by the ebb and flow of this underground sea. They viewed themselves as part of a much greater balance of nature and, although human beings were not in total control, they had a responsibility to maintain that balance through lifestyle and devotion.

▼ The Southeastern Culture Area

Clear across the continent, the Native American tribes of the territory later to become the southeastern United States also believed that their present world was a great flat island, though suspended by four cords from the sky and resting precariously on the surface of the sea. Originally there was only the world of the sky and the underworld. The underworld was a world of chaos, while the upperworld of the sky was orderly and stable. Ghosts and monsters inhabited the underworld, while the world of the sky had many of the same features as the present world (although larger beings, larger homes, chiefs, and councils were not subject to the same limitations imposed on humans). The present world, a realm created later than the others, stood between stability and chaos. While it is difficult to recreate Southeastern tribal belief before the Europeans arrived, the Sun seems to have been important in this Native American belief system, and the sacred fire derived from the Sun was an essential part of tribal ceremony. Likewise, among early groups, the Moon held a kinship with the Sun.

Most of the Native American tribes of the Southeast lived in villages of a few hundred people. Towns of several thousand persons, however, were not uncommon. In chapter one we saw the effects of the Mississippian Culture. The Cherokee, Chickasaw, Choctaw, and Creek were the influential tribes before European arrival (the Seminoles arrived later). At this time the Cherokee was the largest tribe, but the Creek (a confederacy of tribes) wielded the greatest political influence. Rectangular pole houses with woven twig walls covered with a mixture of moist clay and grass were popular. Some had gabled roofs, were two stories high, and had several rooms.

In addition to vast pine forests, the plant life in the Southeast was abundant. The Cherokee used over 800 species of plants for medicine, food, and craftwork. Maize (Native American corn) was the most prominent crop planted, and important festivals surrounded its growing cycle. The subsistence farming on small tracts of land cultivated other culinary delights, including melons, strawberries, beans, squash, potatoes, pumpkins, and peas. Deer was the most prominent animal hunted, usually with sharpened arrows and a bow strung with animal tendon; but southeastern natives highly respected animal spirits and hunted sparingly. Each family was required to cultivate enough crops to feed their family (when supplemented by hunting deer, game birds, bison, and so on), and was expected to add a small portion to the community storehouse for emergencies.

For many of these Native Americans, clans based upon female lineage governed affiliations (later making children of European fathers and Native American mothers full members of the mother's village). Even though women were honored as such and held definite economic power through homes and lands, this does not mean that women controlled the politics of the southeastern tribes. Men made the important tribal decisions, and men became leaders and were appointed to tribal councils. And yet a woman's brother often taught her son, and the rules of kinship and propriety were complex. For example, a widow was expected to marry her husband's brother, and a widower was expected to marry his wife's sister.

The importance of maize and the sacred fire of the Sun came together in the Green Maize Feast, the harvest ceremony, and the Great New Moon Feast, the new year ceremony. The village gathered together in sacred dance and solemn drumming for a celebration of the new year that lasted for days. Members of the village prepared themselves by fasting in order to allow the food from the old year to pass from their bodies. Houses and public buildings were thoroughly cleaned as well. In the evening, reenacting ancient tribal lore, village members danced around a large fire. At dawn they marched single file into the council house to offer ears of maize and bits of produce to the sacred fire. The villagers then went to the river to bathe ritually and cleanse themselves from the spiritual and physical pollution the year had wrought. Old hatreds were to be set aside, and a new year was welcomed as the sacred fire of the village was extinguished and rekindled.

Before the arrival of the Europeans, it appears that the southeastern tribes shunned both war and excessive hunting. There was a high value placed on all life, and a premium placed on human life. The loss of one warrior caused much grief and mourning throughout the Native American community. Tribal disputes, frustrations, and tensions were mollified through a love for games and competitive sports. Sports were highly valued in southeastern Native American culture, and every village had its game fields. Men and women sometimes played together in village games, and a fierce competition developed between the male teams of clans and tribes. Training was rigorous, and Native American competition included physical, psychological, and spiritual preparation.

While lacrosse is a modern version of only one of the traditional games of the Southeast, the most popular sport before the arrival of the Europeans was Chungke. In this game spears were tossed at a rolling stone disk, approximately five inches in diameter and with a hole in the center. In a carefully prepared ball field, level and smooth, the disk was rolled down the center. Staying a prescribed distance away, the two contestants from each team tried to throw their spears closest to where the stone would stop or be stopped. Rules varied among tribes and during various centuries, but the game of Chungke was still being played in the twentieth century by Native American tribes throughout the United States. Games and the spiritual ceremonies that accompanied them were deeply entrenched in southeastern Native American culture, and sports played an important part in physical healing, festivals, funerals, and ceremonial occasions of all kinds before the European arrival.

▼ The Longhouse of the Northeast

Although Native Americans of the Southeast were sometimes viewed as sports fanatics, and their love of games misinterpreted by Europeans, both the Algonkians and Iroquoians of the Northeast claim with pride that their tribes were the first to invent and to play lacrosse, one of the old-est games still in existence. Unlike the southeastern tribes, these Native Americans of the Northeast were on the verge of being destroyed by intertribal warfare before the arrival of the Europeans. The formation of the League of Five Nations of the Iroquois (see chapter one) was an attempt to obtain peace and to protect members against outsiders.

The Cayuga, Mohawk, Oneida, Onondaga, and Seneca tribes involved in this *Ganonsyoni*, "The Lodge Extended Lengthwise," exhibited cultural patterns shared by other tribes of the Northeast. The multifamily longhouse had been cen-tral to individual tribal development since the 1100s. A typ-ical longhouse was approximately 25 feet wide, 80 feet long, and contained three to five fireplaces. Around each fireplace two families would share a two apartment module facing the fire. A hallway ran the length of the building. In some Mohawk villages multifamily longhouses grew as long as 200 feet. Sapling posts bent over at the top were lashed together to form an arbor-type roof, and slabs of bark were lashed to the frame. The longhouse was built on a platform above the ground to help prevent dampness, and floors were covered with mats and furs. With firewood stacked near the doors at the end and storage areas within, the longhouse was the phys-ical trademark of many Northeast tribal villages.

The longhouse also symbolized the social structure and communal sharing of these tribes. The family unit was rec-ognized and valued, the cornerstone unit being the wife, hus-band, and children sharing a fire. Like many Native Ameri-can groups around the land, Iroquoian society was organized matrilineally. Unlike some other Native American regions, however, women of the Northeast exercised political as well as economic power. Although the villages and towns were governed by men, women had a key role in choosing the lead-ers. Senior women privately caucused to make their selection for the members of the male tribal council and to solidify their support for a chief. Men spoke publicly and made the formal decisions, but disregarding the viewpoint of the women behind the scenes could quickly cost a man his political position.

Before the arrival of the Europeans, many of the Native American tribes of the Northeast had developed a culture based on horticulture, hunting, fishing, and gathering. A slash and burn type of agriculture was used, and (as in so many regions) maize, beans, and squash were principal crops. The duties of men and women were narrowly prescribed. Women were the primary agriculturalists, while men were responsible for hunting and fishing. And yet sharing among members of the community was extensive. There was little (if any) perception of private property or sole ownership among families of this Native American community. At first, even in the political realm, multiple chiefs were appointed within large villages or designated from smaller villages to govern over a territory. The Native Americans of the Northeast lived in highly fortified villages composed of numbers of bark longhouses, and as their population grew, each village moved toward increased centralization of political power.

Although Algonkian settlements never reached the size of the larger Iroquoian towns, they too moved toward increased fortification of their once open villages. Algonkians seemed to have placed more emphasis on hunting and fishing, making full use of their access to the Atlantic ocean inlets and the thick forests that surrounded them. For example, Algonkians who occupied the valley of the Delaware River lived in village bands of a few hundred members, some of their multifamily longhouses over 100 feet in length. Large sections of chestnut bark six feet high covered the hickory pole frame of the Delaware longhouse. Log and tree fortification required such longhouse winter settlements to be closer together than the once open and scattered smaller dwellings. And yet, the earlier one-room domed shelters (*wigwams*) continued to be used for summer hunting forays or mobile village excursions. In 1600, Delaware tribal groups had a population approaching 10,000, but the arrival of Europeans devastated their original tribal lands and scattered them to western New York, Wisconsin, Kansas, Oklahoma, and southern Ontario, Canada. Algonkian tribes in the Northeast were not able to withstand both the European onslaught and the Iroquoian Confederation, losing all to the white settlers.

The tribes of the Northeast believed in a Creator who fashioned the earth for human use and enjoyment. The world of the spirit was intertwined with the world of the physical. One's obligation was to follow the path of ancient family traditions, and the tried and tested ceremonies of the longhouse community. Tribal spiritual guides helped Native American men and women to follow the proper path. The prophet, the storyteller, the ritual keeper, and the chanter were respected members of the community. Visions and dreams served significant spiritual functions, connecting the present world with the past and the future. At death, it was believed, the soul began a long journey westward to a point where the sky lifts. After a series of ordeals, admittance was gained into the sky world where the dead reside.

In their misunderstanding of the religion and culture of Native Americans of the Northeast, the Puritans tried to justify their slaughter of Algonkian tribes by characterizing them as nomads of nature, while characterizing comparable Iroquoian settlements as "civilized nations." Nevertheless, even the Northeast Iroquoian tribes would soon suffer from the European onslaught. And yet the traditions of the longhouse survived in the memory of these Native Americans. When Native American religious revival based on the revelations of the prophet Handsome Lake occurred among the Seneca in southwestern New York in 1799, it was appropriately called the Longhouse Religion.

▼ Bison and the Black Hills

By the time the Lewis and Clark Expedition reached the territory surrounding the Black Hills, the Lakota Sioux (or Teton Sioux, see chapter one) had moved west and were firmly entrenched in this Prairie-Plains region. The explorers tried to explain to these Native Americans that a fledgling republic called the United States of America had "purchased" 830,000 acres west of the Mississippi River (including the entire Sioux lands) from the French for 15 million dollars. Lewis and Clark then wrapped a newborn Lakota Sioux child in an American flag to symbolize the U.S. citizenship now "conferred upon" the Sioux people. One thing the Sioux were sure of, however, was that neither the French nor the United States controlled their homeland. They had rarely met a European. The explorers and their president, Thomas Jefferson, may have thought that the United States doubled its territory with the purchase of the vast "Louisiana Territory" in April of 1803, but the Lakota Sioux were not impressed. In turn, Meriwether Lewis penned ugly comments about the Tetons in his journal that would stereotype them in the minds of Europeans for centuries.

While the tribes of the Northeast had to confront Europeans during the colonial period, the Sioux were located in the interior lands of the continent and had avoided the bloodshed. But European immigration had a direct effect on the Sioux and their earlier homeland in the Minnesota and Iowa woodlands. European traders had sold guns to one of the Sioux tribes' ancient enemies, the Chippewa. Time and time again European muskets wielded by the Chippewa defeated valiant Sioux warriors brandishing bows and arrows, slowly forcing the Sioux people to move westward. Gunpowder and the gun would have as drastic an effect on Lakota Sioux life as would the horse.

The Lakota Sioux were divided into seven bands: Black-feet, Brule, Hunkpapa, Miniconjou, Oglala, Sans Arc, and Two Kettle. The Prairie-Plains region in which they had settled had herds containing millions of bison. Related to the ox or cow, the bison stood 5 and a half to 6 feet at the shoulder, had a shaggy mane, humped back, and short horns. Often called the American buffalo, this animal provided meat and hides for the Sioux, replacing the diet of fish and forest game of the woodlands. A century before the Lewis and Clark Expedition the Lakota Sioux began following the bison on their seasonal migration from the north to the south. They developed a portable *tipi* to drag along with them on these excursions. At first, dogs that the Sioux raised and cherished had helped with the travels, pulling loads and patrolling the camp. However, these Native Americans soon found that the pinto, a white-patched wild pony descended from the Spanish explorers' horses, could revolutionize their travel. By the 1700s millions of pintos roamed the Prairie-Plains region, and they gave the Native Americans a new mobility and unprecedented speed on their hunts and during battle. Gaining access to guns as well the Sioux enlarged and protected their new homeland.

It was Standing Bull who led the Sioux into the Black Hills, an area presently in S.W. South Dakota and N.E. Wyoming that rises thousands of feet above the miles of flat grasslands below. The great leader knew that here his people could find shelter and protection in the crevices, canyons, and pine forests. The highest peaks of the Black Hills rise seven thousand feet above sea level. The Lakota Sioux learned to appropriate these lands just as they had continued to survive on the hundreds of miles of prairie grasslands they traversed. In the process, they became the popular expression of the Native American: tall, muscular, brave, alert, nomadic, a possible bloodbrother, a worthy adversary, with eagle-feather headdresses, tipis, and campsites dotting the Prairie-Plains. Indeed, the Lakota lifestyle adapted to the seasons. In response to the harsh winter that approached, small extended family campsites with food, water, and shelter were built as early as October. These dispersed clans would spend their time passing on the oral traditions of their ancestors to their children; honoring the elderly as they shared their wisdom about medicinal plants, plain's survival, and hunting techniques; and sharing quality time with family through activities of happiness, times of worship, and a variety of games. In the spring, as the buffalo herds feasted on tall prairie grass, the families would join together in vast camps of brightly colored blankets and tipis to hunt and worship together as a people. Young braves would prove their prowess and courage. Ceremonies abounded in a camp that was a beehive of activity. Men, women, boys, and girls danced and sang to the Great Spirit (*Wakan Tanka*). The Black Hills that rose majestically against the deep blue sky became a sacred space for a proud people.

As other Native American tribes were encountering Europeans in the seventeenth and eighteenth centuries, trying to maintain their ancient lifestyles in the midst of an immigrating hostile White culture, the Lakota Sioux had a century of respite. The explorers had labelled the Prairie-Plains area a "Great Desert," inhospitable to human habitation. The land was believed to be unfit for agriculture, and it appeared there was little of worth for European exploitation. The U.S. Government declared the Prairie-Plains "Indian Country," and proclaimed to eastern tribes that they must give up their tribal lands and settle there. In the process, the Sioux would become the symbol of "Indianness." And yet, as has been shown in this chapter, European perceptions were only caricatures. A diverse and dynamic Native American culture was present in this land before the "conquerors" arrived.

▼ Native American Worldview

Before the advent of writing, groups of families or clans descended from a common ancestor flourished throughout North and South America. These tribes, composed of preliterate peoples with marvelous memorization skills, embraced religion as a way of life. While these tribal societies are sometimes called "primitive," this modern value-laden term was actually coined by a technological society that would find it difficult to survive as these tribes did. Hunting, gathering, and fishing peoples have always required special skills to subsist in a hostile environment. Such intelligence, sensitivity to nature, and foresight needed to survive on marginal land have been lost in our scientifically oriented, automated world. Western technological societies have cultivated not only a different orientation but also a different set of values. Ironically and tragically, modernity's excessive interest in wealth and self, widespread pollution, and misuse of natural resources have shown the mindset of a European-oriented civilization to be at times simple, rough, and "uncivilized," consonant with the common association of the word *primitive*. Because of this failure, the respect of tribal religion for nature and the centrality of conservation in the society of oral peoples have something to teach modern citizens in a highly technological community.

Most Native Americans had no concept of private ownership of land. No one could "own" that which the primary holy force held together. Furthermore, nature was permeated with divinity, and a variety of spirits worked both good and evil, sustaining all things that had been created by the Great

Spirit and protecting the interests of nature itself. Harmony with nature and peace with the everpresent, willful, human-like spirits was sought through traditional ceremonies. Some tribes believed that nature would cease to exist if they did not practice their religion. Certain qualities permeate this Native American life: respect for family, the preciousness of children, honoring the elderly, pride in craftsmanship, the value of working for a purpose with one's hands, listening to one's neighbor, being discrete (especially when another's honor and dignity are concerned), taking time to be introspective and contemplative about the mysteries of the universe, and valu-ing oral traditions that engender humbleness, sharing, and laughter.

For the Native American, as with so many tribal societies around the world, the primary goal was to be in harmony with nature, and spiritual specialists functioned as mediators in this supernatural drama. White settlers called them "medi-cine men," because they were struck with their function in healing. Indeed, Native Americans introduced many helpful drugs and medicines to white settlers. But the powers of these "medicine men" also included divination and prophetic inter-pretation. Many tribes taught that a boy entering maturity must seek the help of a guiding spirit, often in his *vision quest* ceremony. Important in the vision quest of some tribes and in the psyche of Native American religion today is the reve-latory nature of dreams and visions. Sometimes a young man was sent to encounter such a vision by leaving the tribe for a period of days and seeking a guiding spirit through fasting and ritual. Throughout life such visions were important on the eve of great decisions and great battles, and they contribute to the very personal character of the religion of the Native American.

The ceremonies performed by the tribe's holy men and women, however, were not to take the place of an individual's heartfelt worship. Although ancient specialists in spirit manipulation were often called upon, each member of the tribe was expected to dance, sing, perform rituals, and through visions and dreams make contact with the Great Spirit. This personal worship, as well as an individual's rite of passage, provided harmony in the present life, a harmony that was the seat of joy and happiness. A harmonious relationship with departed ancestors, reverence for the land, and traditional practice of religious ceremonies were instinctively engendered by a close-knit community. Disharmony with nature and the spirits led to disaster, and misfortune was often blamed on evil ones.

These attitudes of harmony and ecological balance are in distinct contrast to modern urban concepts of power through possessions and status, and a decimated Native American population currently struggles against total annihilation by a technological society with other values. As we shall see in the next chapter, it is a struggle that has historic roots and entangling webs that span centuries.

▲▼▲ 3 ▲▼▲

THE HISTORY OF PAIN

Remains of Lost Bird, a young Sioux woman, were exhumed in the month of July, 1991, from a graveyard in Hanford, California, and transferred by horse-drawn wagon in solemn ceremony from Porcupine Butte to a mass grave of hundreds of Native Americans. The mass grave contained the remains of Sioux men, women, and children massacred by the U.S. Seventh Cavalry at Wounded Knee in 1890. Now Lost Bird had joined them.

In 1890, as a four-month-old baby, Lost Bird had been miraculously found alive after the massacre, crying in her dead mother's frozen blood. Like so many Sioux women that day Lost Bird's mother had sought to protect her child with her last ounce of life. The young child was taken away and raised in the Nebraska home of General Leonard Wright Colby (some say as a "trophy of war"). Her name was changed to Marguerite Elizabeth Colby, and the Colby family attempted to "civilize" Lost Bird. The white community never accepted the child, however, and she ended up traveling as an extra with Buffalo Bill's Wild West Show. After a lifetime of abuse and rejection Lost Bird died in poverty at the age of twenty-nine.

To many Native Americans, Lost Bird symbolizes the tens of thousands of Sioux children taken from their families and adopted by families of European descent. A photograph of General Colby holding the young child reveals a look of perplexity and sadness on Lost Bird's face. She often spoke of returning "home," but did not accomplish that feat during her short lifetime. Now, a century after her birth, her Sioux relatives performed the Morning Star ceremony, a traditional "releasing" of her spirit.

Today, in her honor, the Lost Bird Society seeks to reunite Native Americans adopted as children with their tribal relatives. Lost Bird herself remains a symbol of the disruption of Native American families during "the history of pain."

▼ Disease

Whenever and wherever Europeans came in contact with Native Americans, change occurred. The most immediate change in Native American life stemmed from the introduction of European diseases to the American continent. Virtually every time Native Americans had contact with Europeans they were plagued with microorganisms carrying smallpox, influenza, measles, chicken pox, malaria, and other diseases. Because Native Americans had passed through Arctic regions and environmental conditions in which these pathogens were nearly nonexistent, they had no immunity to the microorganisms the Europeans passed on to them. Extended contact meant death and depopulation for the American tribes (or "nations"). A half century after Christopher Columbus "discovered" the "New World," millions of Native Americans had died from European-transmitted diseases.

Such disease and subsequent death plagued Native American communities well into the nineteenth century. This depopulation (as high as 90 percent in some villages) destabilized Native American community structures and patterns, mercilessly altering tribal lifestyles. Pueblo society in the Southwest, for example, had been continually decimated since the 1500s by epidemics and warfare precipitated by Spanish conquest. The Spanish themselves estimated that by 1638 more than 20,000 Pueblo men, women, and children had died from epidemics since the Spanish conquest in the 1540s. In 1780 a year-long plague of smallpox alone killed over 5,000 additional Native American villagers in New Mexico, many of them in the Hopi pueblos.

Across the continent in the Chesapeake region of the eastern seaboard similar epidemics took their toll in the latter 1500s and early 1600s. In 1616 English fishermen triggered an epidemic among New England tribes, resulting in the deaths of tens of thousands of Native Americans within the year. Between 1617 and 1619, the Powhatan tribes were decimated by European-spread disease. In the aftermath of this pathogenic infection the area around Plymouth was nearly depopulated.

In the 1630s epidemics struck the Hurons, Mohawks, Petun, Wenro, Neutrals, and Nipissings in the East. During the winter of 1636-1637, the Nipissing tribespeople lost seventy men, women, and children to disease while wintering in Huronia, a number that escalated when they returned to their homeland the following spring. The population of the Huron confederacy was cut in half to 10,000 by the epidemic. Smallpox raged among the Senecas in the winter of 1640–1641. The Iroquois lost over 1,000 in 1662, after a decade of sporadic epidemic outbreak. In face of such microscopic onslaught, the Iroquoian Confederacy seems to have been able to maintain little more than half of its population after its contact with Europeans. In 1677 the Delawares remembered a smallpox epidemic in their grandparents' day, their parents' day, and in their current experience, each precipitated by European contact.

Among the Native Americans of the Southeast, European-originated epidemics took their toll. For instance, in 1738 a smallpox infestation killed one-half of the Cherokee population. Although sheltered from early explorers, Native Americans of the Northwest Coast began to suffer epidemics of smallpox, scarlet fever, malaria, measles, influenza, and whooping cough soon after European contact. Smallpox seems to have been the first to strike these tribes in the 1770s, exacting a heavy toll in human life.

▼ Slavery

Europeans were involved in kidnapping and enslaving Native Americans from an early date. In a letter dated July 8, 1524, the Italian explorer, Giovanni da Verrazano, wrote to his benefactor, King Francis I of France, that his crew kidnapped a Native American child from an old woman and also attempted to abduct "a beautiful woman of tall stature." The young Native American woman screamed, however, scaring the sailors into abandoning their plan and leaving her on shore. At the beginning of the 1600s, the Portuguese explorer Gasper Corte Real kidnapped over fifty Native Americans and sold them into slavery.

In addition, English expeditions sporadically attacked and kidnapped Native Americans on the East Coast. In 1502 explorer Sebastian Cabot put on display in England three Native Americans he had captured during his Arctic voyage. Even the famed princess, Pocahontas, initially was kidnapped from her village; and Squanto, the Wampanoag tribesman who gave important assistance to the Pilgrims when they landed, had earlier been sold into slavery in Europe and then made his way back in time to welcome the Mayflower. By the time Squanto returned to the Cape Cod area, nearly his whole tribe had died of plague. In 1614, one of John Smith's captains captured a score of Native Americans, took them back to Spain, and sold them into slavery. John Smith himself advocated deception and intimidation toward Native Americans, recommending unrestrained violence to keep the tribes in line.

The Puritans of New England punished the Pequot tribespeople for their opposition to European settlement by killing hundreds of Pequot men, women, and children and by selling hundreds of others into slavery. The captive male Pequots were sold and shipped to the West Indies while the Puritans made slaves at home of the tribe's women and children. This enslavement of the Native Americans by colonists of Massachusetts Bay occurred at the very same time that the Puritans were attempting to organize a "holy" colony based on the dictates of the Bible. The Puritan colonies would soon become the lucrative commercial hub of the famous triangle between Africa and the West Indies, a "Golden Triangle" that would bring suffering, degradation, and death to millions of Africans.

The new territory of Carolina began a concerted effort to enslave Native Americans, kidnapping or buying them to sell in the profitable slave trade with New England and the West Indies. Slavery became a central component in the Carolina economy during the early years of its development. In Virginia, in 1676, the Assembly legalized the enslavement of Native Americans, paralleling the process Virginia followed in its enslavement of Africans. Many times enslavement was rationalized on the assumption that Native Americans were "barbarous infidels" and needed "thinning out." In reality,

Native Americans inhabited a land that European settlers coveted.

▼ Colonial Relationships

Lack of respect and even hatred toward Native Americans were bred into each progressive generation of European settlers in the colonies. When Native Americans welcomed and helped European settlers they were viewed as naive adolescents who did not deserve the territory, and who could be manipulated and cheated at will. Whenever Native Americans stood up for their rights, fought the Europeans and won in battle, their successful attacks were used as an excuse by Europeans to bring in larger militias to slaughter tribes. For every positive portrayal of tribal life in the 1600s and 1700s, a hundred negative portrayals were penned by European explorers, traders, and settlers. So all-pervading were the negative accounts that scholars have a difficult time today separating fact from fiction. In addition, original European intentions were mixed and complicated.

The European directors of the Dutch West India Company, for example, had carefully planned their New Amsterdam colony on Manhattan Island. They intended to foster cordial relations with the Native Americans and develop a strong network of trade. In their directives they called the tribes "Lord Sachems" and stressed that agreements between all parties (Native American and Dutch) must be obtained. Colonial lands that made up the New Netherlands were to be purchased from their rightful owners. Native Americans in the New York area responded with good will and acts of kindness. The actual Dutch settlers and their leaders, however, exploited the Native Americans, cheated them without even hiding their contempt for the tribes, and cavalierly dismissed them as "wild men."

On February 25, 1642, Dutch Governor Willem Kieft, in his continuing effort to expel Native Americans from the area of New Amsterdam, led soldiers on a night raid, repaying the Native American kindness with a cruel slaughter. Over 120 men, women, and children were mutilated and killed in their wigwams. According to Dutch reports, Native American women were cut open by the swords of the Dutch soldiers and babies were bayoneted. Native American men had their hands cut off, and slashed children were thrown into the river to drown. The village was burned to the ground. The Dutch committee investigating the horror called it an "unnecessary, bloody and ruinous war." Although the Dutch decreed that no war should be waged against Native Americans without the express knowledge of the king and queen, the damage had been done. Native Americans rose in righteous indignation.

In New England, where Puritans sought to conform the world to God's ideals and to spread God's love, one would think that coexistence with the Native American communities would have been possible. Unfortunately the Puritan view of the Bible was clouded by their European culture. European law dictated that land that was not settled according to "civilized norms" was actually "unoccupied." The Puritan Governor of the Massachusetts Bay Colony, John Winthrop, wrote that Native Americans in New England did not "enclose" the land and did not "improve" the land with cattle. In the view of Governor Winthrop and with the blessing of European culture this meant that he and his Puritan community had "a Natural Right" to New England. He did mention in his papers, however, that Native Americans should have land "sufficient for their use," but at the same time firmly maintained that his Puritan people "may lawfully take the rest, there being more than enough for them and us." In these particulars European patterns of civilization seemed to dictate Puritan concepts of God's Law.

Rampant epidemics and disease among Native Americans did not help to ameliorate the Puritan view toward them. Not only were the tribes of New England in their weakened condition unable to stem the European settlement onslaught, but the Puritans viewed the death and destruction of the tribes as God's judgment upon them. For Winthrop and others, it was "God's Will" that the Puritans inhabit and "subdue" the land. Little wonder that Native Americans surrounding the New England colonies were viewed as savage "subjects."

When Roger Williams argued that his Puritan neighbors had illegally and shamefully stolen Native American land and would have to answer to God for their actions, Governor Winthrop replied that the land was God's and it was God's right to take it from the Native Americans and "give it" to the Puritans. "Who shall control God or God's terms," John Winthrop responded. The Massachusetts magistrates ceremonially burned Roger Williams' writings against Puritan usurpation of Native American land and soon banished Williams from the colony (see chapter five). Later, Increase Mather, Puritan pastor of Boston's North Church from 1664–1723, and rector of Harvard University from 1685–1701, would write: "Lord God of Our Father hath given us for a rightful possession the lands of Heathen People amongst whom we live."

In the Chesapeake area of Virginia, as in Massachusetts Bay, cordial relations between Native Americans and English settlers soon degenerated into bickering and violence. Early European settlers had found the local tribes to be "most gentle, loving, and faithful, void of all guile and treason." Native Americans helped these settlers to survive the harsh winters by bringing them food and teaching them to live on the land. And yet Europeans raided tribal food supplies and used guns to underscore their superiority. The colonial assembly in Jamestown, Virginia, decreed that any settler would be hanged if he or she gave Native Americans "any shooting piece, shot, powder, or any arms, offensive or defensive." ·

Between 1610 and 1622 nearly 10,000 settlers streamed into Virginia, and violence mounted between the original inhabitants and the European invaders. An insatiable desire for tobacco drove the English to appropriate ever larger tracts of Native American land. Tobacco depleted the soil, and Europeans moved on to fresh acreage. War ensued. Early skirmishes were won by Native Americans. The growing number of European colonists, however, soon overran the depleted tribes of Virginia and began to win every battle. By 1700 the Native American population in the Chesapeake area dwindled to less than one thousand. Respect and consideration for the local tribes dwindled as well.

When the French and English vied for the eastern half of the North American continent in the latter seventeenth and early eighteenth centuries, Native Americans were caught in the crossfire. Like the other European nations France had not been able to settle colonists in large numbers as England had done. Tensions increased as over a million English colonists strengthened England's hold on the continent and interfered with France's lucrative trade in furs and goods. Realizing the importance of Native Americans to a successful effort, England created the Indian Department in 1755 and appointed an experienced New York diplomat in Native American affairs, Sir William Johnson, as superintendent of the northern territories. Both England and France tried to use tribes against each other, wooing Native Americans with promises and treaties. Finally, in the Seven Years' War (1756–1763; also known as the "French and Indian War" or the "Great War for Empire"), the English totally defeated the French and took control of the eastern sector of North America (except for New Orleans) from the Mississippi River to the Atlantic Ocean.

The English government issued the Royal Proclamation of October 7, 1763, initiating a new policy with Native Americans. A vast Indian Territory was created between the Appalachian Mountains in the east and the Mississippi River to the west. Colonists were not to live in that territory and Europeans who had homes there were ordered to return to the East. Special licenses had to be obtained by Europeans even to trade in the area. Although England issued stern decrees to its colonial governors to abide by this new "racial boundary," it was unable to enforce the new policy. England staggered in debt from the Seven Years' War and had increasing difficulty in getting its American colonies to help pay for past and present expenses through taxes and trade. Settlers and land speculators continued to push enmasse into the newly-proclaimed area reserved for Native American tribes, and warfare flared as inland tribes between the Appalachian Mountains and the Mississippi River served notice that they would not relinquish their homelands without a fight.

The Revolutionary War between the thirteen American colonies and Great Britain interrupted England's effort to preserve the territorial integrity of the inland tribes. A number of the officials in Britain's Indian Department, including Sir William Johnson, remained loyal to the King of England. They helped enlist Native American support for the British. Native Americans also realized that the American revolutionaries were made up of farmers and frontiersmen who encroached on their homelands and attempted to destroy the Native American way of life. Therefore, during the American Revolution, Native Americans often sided with the British, feverishly attacking the colonial frontiersmen who had destroyed their villages from western New York to the Ohio valley. Sealing their fate with British fortunes, Native Americans and their opposition would not be forgotten by the newly created United States of America. Old hatreds would die hard, and justice would be sacrificed to expediency and greed.

Although Native American culture was resilient during the Colonial Period and resisted drastic alterations in its ancient traditions, it was painfully assaulted by foreign governments and European settlers. At best, most Europeans thought they were purchasing private property when Native Americans were only attempting to show them hospitality. At worst, Europeans knowingly stole Native American tribal lands.

▼ From Revolution to Constitution

At the time of the Declaration of Independence, the young Cherokee warrior Dragging Canoe joined with the Shawnee chief Cornstalk in fighting against the Americans. Upset with American encroachment on Cherokee lands, Dragging Canoe launched raids against white settlements in the area that would later become eastern Tennessee. By the end of July, 1776, nearly the whole Cherokee nation and its 2500 warriors were at war with the newly-formed United States of America. Although Cherokee towns would be burned and Cherokee chiefs would be forced to sign treaties with the new American nation by the end of the year, Dragging Canoe would lead opposition forces composed of hundreds of Native Americans (known as the Chickamauga Cherokees) until his death in 1792.

When a militia force of 1800 patriots from Virginia ravaged and burned Cherokee towns in October 1776, Thomas Jefferson applauded their efforts. Noting that the revolutionary struggle with Britain was "too serious and too great" to allow an "Indian" uprising, Jefferson wrote that he hoped "the Cherokees will now be driven beyond the Mississippi": the "invariable consequence" of opposing the United States of America. In reality, however, Native Americans who fought on the American side during the Revolutionary War or stayed out of the struggle as requested suffered similar devastation and loss of their lands.

In the Treaty of Paris—signed in September, 1783, between Great Britain and the United States of America—the Revolutionary War officially ended. Britain, however, refused to protect Native Americans in the treaty, allowing even their Native American allies to suffer the full consequences of loyalty to defeated Great Britain. The promised and legally proclaimed "Indian Country" between the Appalachian Mountains and the Mississippi River was not even mentioned by negotiators. To complicate matters, seven of the thirteen colonies claimed to control lands west of the Appalachians, dividing in parallel territories the Indian Country. The other six colonies argued that these lands should be shared in common in the new confederation.

In the Treaty of Paris England agreed to recognize the independence of the thirteen colonies, to remove her forces, and to set the western boundary of the United States at the Mississippi River. The United States promised to honor prewar debts and to restore the property of *white* colonists who had remained loyal to England. The month following this treaty, the Congress of the United States of America published a report specifying that Native Americans had forfeited their lands when they sided with the British. Each tribe was to be treated as a nation and all boundaries would be set at the discretion and "compassion" of the United States.

Government agents explained to each tribe that they were to acquiesce to the dictated terms or watch the extermination of their people. Major General Richard Butler, for example, told tribal representatives in a meeting at Fort Finney, Kentucky, that the "destruction of your women and children or their future happiness depends on your present choice." On August 7, 1786, the Congress established two departments of Indian affairs: a northern department with jurisdiction west of the Hudson River and north of the Ohio River, and a south-ern department with jurisdiction south of the Ohio River. Working with the Articles of Confederation as its guide, the Confederation Congress established the first federal "Indian reservations" the same year. Realizing that it did not have the armed forces to control all Native Americans north and south of the Ohio River, the Congress decided to pacify the Native Americans to the south and to concentrate on negotiations and a show of force north of the Ohio River.

In 1785 the Congress enacted a land ordinance providing for the systematic survey and inevitable sale of lands west of New York and Pennsylvania, and north of the Ohio River. Townships six miles square were laid out in rectangular grids throughout the area that would become the present-day Mid-west. These townships were in turn subdivided into lots of 640 acres each. These were to be sold to white settlers and land speculators in an effort to reduce the national debt. In addition, Congress passed the Northwest Ordinance in 1787, providing for the political organization of the same area. The United States of America was poised for a massive expansion into Native American lands.

A clause of the Northwest Ordinance related directly to the treatment of Native Americans. Although it has been labelled the "Utmost Good Faith" clause, it underscores the betrayal that Native Americans would feel when they real-ized that the United States of America was bent on creating an "empire" in a world of empires —an empire at the expense of Native American tribes. Declaring that the articles of the Northwest Ordinance would "forever remain unalterable," the Congress promised in 1787 that

> The utmost good faith shall always be observed towards the Indians; their land and property shall never be taken from

them without their consent; and, in their property, rights, and
liberty, they shall never be invaded or disturbed, unless in just
and lawful wars authorized by Congress, but laws founded in
justice and humanity, shall from time to time be made for pre-
venting wrongs being done to them, and for preserving peace
and friendship with them.

The loophole that Congress would employ in this clause is
found in the phrase "unless in just and lawful wars authorized
by Congress." Such wars would be instigated by the actions of
the United States of America and its representatives
throughout the next century.

Protection of Native Americans, as well as the "justice" and
"humanity" mentioned in the clause would be sacrificed to
political expediency. A plethora of treaties were signed
between 1783 and 1786, very few of them with chiefs or leaders of confederacies. Although the Intercourse Act of 1790
clearly states that Congress must approve any treaties made
between state governments and Native American tribes, few
state officials and white entrepreneurs bothered to adhere to
such laws. The phrase concerning "land and property" that
shall "never be taken" from Native Americans "without their
consent" was made a sham even before the Northwest Ordinance was signed into law. Other laws for the protection of
Native Americans would be neglected as well. Sadly, throughout most of American history "utmost good faith" has not been
practiced with regard to Native American communities.

▼ The Early National Period

On March 4, 1789, the Constitution of the United States
of America took effect. Article I section 8 gave the Congress
the power to "regulate commerce with foreign nations, and
among the several States, and *with the Indian tribes.*" Considered to be outside the Union, Native American tribes were to

be negotiated with as foreign nations, and regulation of trade with them became the exclusive domain of Congress. On August 7, 1789, Congress established the War Department, making "Indian Affairs" one of the functions of the Secretary of War. Noting that there were serious conflicts between Indian interests and White interests, the Congress used language very close to that used in the Northwest Ordinance.

> The utmost good faith shall always be observed towards the Indians; their land and their property shall never be taken from them without their consent and their property, rights and liberty shall never be invaded or disturbed, unless in just and lawful wars authorized by Congress, but laws founded in justice and humanity shall from time to time be made, for preventing wrongs being done to them, and for preserving peace and friendship with them.

The Louisiana Purchase in 1801 doubled the territory of the United States and placed tens of thousands of additional Native Americans west of the Mississippi River at the mercy of "the utmost good faith" of the U.S. Congress.

The Founding Fathers spoke often of protecting the rights and liberty of Native Americans. In reality, however, the early governmental leaders of the United States believed that the Native American community would be "civilized" and "assimilated" into the culture of an expanding United States. It was expected that Native Americans would sell their vast lands and merge their interests with the interests of the settlers and immigrants of the new country. When Native American tribes refused to comply with these precepts they were forced into war or tricked into submission by an ever more powerful United States. In either case, they were deprived of tribal lands.

George Washington himself stated that "the gradual extension of our settlements will as certainly cause the savage as the wolf to retire; both beasts of prey though they differ in shape." In the same vein, John Quincy Adams, the son of President John Adams and a future president himself, declared in a speech in 1802: "But what is the right of a huntsman to the forest of a thousand miles over which he has accidentally ranged in quest of prey? Shall the liberal bounties of Providence to the race of man be monopolized by one of ten thousand for whom they were created?" Pointing to the importance of progress and the role of civilization, John Quincy Adams questioned the Native American right of possession to the Land: "Shall the lordly savage not only disdain the virtues and enjoyments of civilization himself, but shall he control the civilization of a world?" Such viewpoints indicate a desire for empire on the North American continent by the Founding Fathers coupled with their lack of respect for tribal society.

During his presidency Thomas Jefferson suggested that Native American leaders should be encouraged to buy on large lines of credit at government trading posts. His hope was that the subsequent large debts incurred would be paid off with tribal lands. Jefferson also supported a movement that encouraged tribes to become farming communities (in an effort to draw them toward "civilization"). A later president, James Monroe, was much more blunt in his approach. Speaking after the War of 1812, a war in which some Native Americans again looked to Great Britain for justice, President Monroe declared in his first annual message to Congress in 1817 that "the earth was given to mankind to support the greatest numbers of which it is capable, and no tribe, or people have a right to withhold from the wants of others more than is necessary for their own support and comfort." Two years later Congress set up a token "Civilization Fund" to educate the Native American in the ways of White society.

Even President Monroe, however, was faced with those who could not reconcile removal of Native Americans from their homelands with the often expressed desire of "civilizing the savage." For example, Congregational minister and Yale graduate Jedidiah Morse was appointed by President Monroe in 1820 to visit border tribes, to survey removal problems, and to devise a plan to advance Native American "civilization and happiness." The 59-year-old Rev. Morse reported to both the president and the secretary of war, John C. Calhoun, that to remove Native Americans from their homes "into a wilderness among strangers, possibly hostile, to live as their neighbors live, by hunting, a state to which they have not been lately accustomed, and which is incompatible with civilization, can hardly be reconciled with the professed object of civilizing them." Nevertheless, in his final message to Congress, President James Monroe outlined a removal policy. He believed (as did many of his colleagues) that the Louisiana Purchase had provided the 827,987 square miles of "empty land" that could become a new "Indian Country." And, it had only cost around 15 million dollars.

While some citizens and philanthropists in the United States attempted to prevent or blunt the inhumane actions of the expanding nation, attitudes toward "progress" and "civilization" steamrolled their humanitarian efforts. As the gentleman politician of the Washington Era gave way to the mass marketing techniques of the national political parties of the Jacksonian Era, it became increasingly important to be photographed in front of a log cabin (even if you owned a mansion!) and to be a hero of "Indian Wars." With the repudiation of intellectual statesmen by voters, a blunter language and more forthright frontier analysis of the "Indian Problem" surfaced. The true feelings and intentions of the American government became much more apparent.

"Humanity has often wept over the fate of the aborigines of this country, and Philanthropy has been long busily employed in devising means to avert it," President Andrew Jackson declared in his Second Annual Message to Congress in 1830 (months after he had signed the Indian Removal Act), "but its progress has never for a moment been arrested, and one by one have many powerful tribes disappeared from the earth." Referring to the do-gooders who would question such progress of European civilization at the expense of Native American civilization, President Jackson argued:

> But true Philanthropy could not wish to see this continent restored to the condition in which it was found by our fore-fathers. What good man would prefer a country covered with forests and ranged by a few thousand savages to our extensive Republic, studded with cities, towns, and prosperous farms, embellished with all the improvements which art can devise or industry execute, occupied by more than twelve million happy people, and filled with all the blessings of liberty, civilization, and religion?

Little wonder that no man in the early national period single-handedly removed more Native Americans from their homes and appropriated more tribal land in his lifetime than did Andrew Jackson. For all of his fame and national appeal Jackson had launched and sustained his political career at the expense of the Native American people. His policies and actions would be duplicated throughout the nineteenth century.

▼ Force and Removal

The War of 1812 appeared to be the last chance for Native Americans to alter the expansionist course of the young United States of America. In the early 1800s a few Native

American leaders realized that without unifying against the white settlers Native Americans stood little chance of protecting homes and land from the European onslaught. In the Indiana Territory, the Shawnee chief Tecumseh and his brother Tenskwatawa attempted to unify the tribes, both North and South. Gaining support from many of the smaller tribes north of the Ohio River, Tecumseh traveled south in 1811 to try to convince the great tribes of the Southeast to join his alliance. Although his mother was Creek, Tecumseh could not convince any of the Southeastern tribes to unify.

Tecumseh's efforts ran counter to the efforts of the Governor of the Indiana Territory, William Henry Harrison (governor from 1800–1813). Born in Virginia, Harrison served as a military officer in the Indian Wars of the Northwest Territory (1791–1794) and was appointed governor in 1800. His policies toward Native Americans were circumscribed by his effort to please fellow Virginian Thomas Jefferson. In Tecumseh's absence Governor Harrison marched a force of one thousand men toward Tecumseh's village. Tecumseh's brother decided to attack first, launching an offensive against Harrison's camp on the Tippecanoe River on November 7, 1811.

By sheer numbers Governor Harrison's forces overwhelmed the Native American onslaught, and moved on to burn Tecumseh's village to the ground. Dubbed a "hero," William Henry Harrison was called "Old Tippecanoe," a slogan that served him well when he successfully ran for president in 1840. It is estimated that between 1802, when President Jefferson oversaw his efforts, and 1814–1815, his appointment by President James Madison as a treaty negotiator, William Henry Harrison concluded treaties with Native Americans that gained the United States over 30 million acres of land. Tecumseh returned to the Indiana Territory, helping the British in their effort to convince northern Native American tribes to join forces with them against the United States. The

British hoped to retain their lucrative North American fur trade by maintaining settlements around the Great Lakes and taking the territory between Canada and the Ohio River. British commanders in North America insisted that they must use Native Americans in their war effort, or the United States would use the tribes to their advantage.

When the War of 1812 broke out between Britain and the United States early British control of Fort Dearborn near Chicago and victory over American forces at Detroit gave the British control of the western end of the Great Lakes. Tecumseh was involved in almost every Native American engagement for the British. The British had promised to allow the Native American tribes to continue occupying the land between Canada and the Ohio River. As in the American Revolution, however, the tides of battle turned in favor of the United States. In the Battle of the Thames (October 5, 1813), William Henry Harrison led a force of 5,000 men east of Detroit into western Ontario and soundly defeated the remnants of British and Native American forces in that area. Tecumseh was killed in the battle.

Tecumseh had argued for political and military unity among Native American tribes, insisting that all previous treaties were invalid, improperly negotiated, and did not represent the interests of the Native American people of North America. With his death and the defeat of the British, Native Americans of the Midwest were once again at the mercy of the United States of America. Although in the Treaty of Ghent the British included Article 9, which obligated the United States to guarantee the same land and status to Native Americans as they had possessed in 1811 (before the War of 1812), the United States government never returned any of the confiscated Native American land.

Southeast

Meanwhile, in the Southeast, Native American peoples chose different paths to protect their culture. Their diverse approaches and lack of unified effort made Tecumseh's warn-ings prophetic. Sadly, whether tribal peoples of the South-east negotiated in good faith, trusted the U.S. government to exercise "utmost good faith," or blatantly chose total war, each Native American group in the Southeast was systemat-ically torn from its land, suffered death and destruction, and had any survivors removed to reservations. Among the Creek warriors a group called the Red Sticks insisted on fighting all white intruders. In 1808 Andrew Jackson, a hotheaded com-mander of the Tennessee militia, begged President Thomas Jefferson to let him "punish" the "ruthless foe."

Ironically, during the War of 1812, Andrew Jackson was not only given the opportunity to crush the Red Sticks with the combined Tennessee and Kentucky militia units of 5,000 men, but he gathered additional forces of hundreds of Chero-kee, Chickasaw, and Choctaw warriors to help him. Jackson employed the usual military techniques of burning Native American villages, destroying tribal crops, and killing village livestock. In addition to these tried measures of weakening the Native American opposition, Jackson's forces weakened the target with cannon fire and wrapped their lines around each village in a net of gunfire. The climactic battle of this Creek War centered on Horseshoe Bend in Alabama in March 1814. More Native Americans died in this battle than in any other single battle in American history (over 800).

Andrew Jackson believed that he had to totally crush Native American pride and tradition. He marched to the most sacred area of the Creek nation, Hickory Ground, and constructed Fort Jackson on the site. Although many in the Creek nation had remained neutral during the fighting and had tried to comply with U.S. demands, Andrew Jackson insisted that the entire Creek nation was responsible for the actions of the militant few. He immediately confiscated 22 million acres of Creek tribal lands, two-thirds of their territory.

Dubbed "Old Hickory," Andrew Jackson was appointed major general in the U.S. Army, was credited for the defeat of the British at the Battle of New Orleans in 1815, and became a national hero (even touring the nation). Within a few years Andrew Jackson had become a symbol of American ingenuity, "a man for the common people." Resolutions in several states called for him to be president. In the Election of 1828 Jackson's new Democratic Party won by a slim margin. One of their slogans against incumbent John Quincy Adams proclaimed: "Who do you want? John Quincy Adams, who quotes the law, or Andy Jackson, who makes the law?"

Indian Removal Act of 1830

Andrew Jackson and other influential government leaders decided that Native Americans should be moved west of the Mississippi River. A few tribes had gone west in the 1790s and several thousand settled in the area of modern-day Arkansas and Missouri. Many of these Native Americans were pushed south into Oklahoma by territorial militias and ever-increasing numbers of white settlers. There they ran into conflict with tribes that already had settled in the area. In most conflicts the U.S. Army was called upon as the final arbiter of force. Stretched thin in the process and rarely used to protect Native American interests, the Army was a poor executor of legislation and directives (especially those that spelled out Native American rights). In addition, although Native American rights were supposed to be protected in courts of law, Native Americans were prosecuted for crimes against

Whites much more frequently than Whites for their crimes against Native Americans.

In 1823 the Supreme Court ruled that Native Americans could not be denied protection of the law ("due process"). Supreme Court Justice John Marshall commented that "absolute ultimate ownership" of tribal lands rested with the United States government. "It has never been contended that the Indian title amounted to nothing," Chief Justice Marshall added, "their right of possession has never been questioned." When the decision was recounted to Andrew Jackson, Jackson declared, "John Marshall has made his decision; let him embrace it." Under Jackson's leadership, and with a large sympathetic block in Congress, the Indian Removal Act was passed on May 28, 1830. President Jackson immediately signed it into law. This legislation authorized the president to set up districts west of the Mississippi River, and to forcibly exchange such districts for Native American land east of the Mississippi. 500,000 dollars was appropriated to carry out the program.

Ironically, it was the most "civilized" of the Native American tribes, the so-called Five Civilized Tribes (Cherokee, Chickasaw, Choctaw, Creek, and Seminole), that suffered the most under this legislation. Many of them had turned to European-style agriculture, some even running plantations that had slaves. Hundreds from their number had volunteered to fight for the United States in the War of 1812. They had used the legislative process and the courts since the early 1800s to make "lasting agreements" and "binding treaties." Now, in one fell swoop, they were forced to leave their homelands. At the end of 1828 the State of Georgia, heartened by the election of Andrew Jackson, declared that within six months all Indians within the state would come under the jurisdiction of Georgia law. To complicate matters gold was found on Cherokee lands in Georgia in 1829.

A classic confrontation between states' rights and federal jurisdiction had erupted, and the whole United States was involved. In a desperate attempt to ward off removal, the Cherokee nation in Georgia appealed to the Supreme Court in its suit against the State of Georgia for violation of Cherokee sovereignty. Chief Justice John Marshall decided, however, that the Cherokee nation was not a foreign nation according to the Constitution, but rather, that Native American tribes were "domestic dependent nations." When missionaries in the Cherokee domain were arrested by the State of Georgia's agents, however, Chief Justice Marshall ruled in favor of the Cherokees. John Marshall wrote of the Native Americans: "America was inhabited by a distinct people, divided into separate nations, independent of each other, and of the rest of the world, and governing themselves by their own laws." The State of Georgia ignored his ruling.

Watching the Cherokee Nation's futile legal effort, the Creek voted in council to accept state jurisdiction in Alabama. Their vote was disregarded, and their tribal council was forced to sign a removal treaty in 1832. Delays in the actual immigration procedure, however, brought conflict between Creeks and anxious whites who invaded their homes. The Creek War broke out in 1836, and the Native Americans were defeated by a combination of federal troops and state volunteers. Chickasaw negotiators quickly sold their eastern lands the same year and moved west without federal force. The Choctaws had arranged in 1830 to give up their lands east of the Mississippi River in exchange for lands west of Arkansas.

The Seminoles in Spanish Florida, who had gone to war in 1817 and were crushed by General Andrew Jackson, made a second stand in 1835. This Second Seminole War would drag on for years, until by 1842 only three hundred Seminoles were left in the Florida territory. One of the famed leaders in battle, Osceola, died as a prisoner in Fort Moultrie. Before burying him, U.S. officers severed his head from his body and displayed it in a "Medical Museum." The United States had forced Spain to cede Florida in 1821 (the treaty was signed in 1819)—now most Native Americans in the area were forced out as well.

Trail of Tears

In 1836 the Senate of the United States and a few Native American leaders who saw no hope of thwarting the removal policy of the United States signed the Treaty of New Echota. This gave the Cherokee Nation two years to move to western territories. The Cherokee tribe was deeply split over the treaty. Leaders such as John Ross, who was one-eighth Cherokee but had earned the lasting respect of his bloodbrothers, insisted that the treaty did not reflect the will of the Cherokee people. General John E. Wool, who had been assigned the task of keeping the Cherokees peaceful, was so appalled at the unfair nature of the treaty and the blatant injustice of the Jackson administration toward Native Americans that he asked to be relieved of his command. Only two thousand Cherokees left voluntarily. Over 15,000 decided to stay on their eastern homelands. Ross and his colleagues went to Washington to lodge protests, to petition Congress, to garner the support of prominent families, and to publicize the plight of Cherokee citizens. An intense debate ensued, led by John Ross, the debonair, well-dressed, educated, Methodist convert and Cherokee leader.

President Jackson remained intransigent. General Winfield Scott of Virginia, a hero of the War of 1812 and the field commander in the Blackhawk War of 1832 and in the Seminole Wars, was appointed superintendent of Cherokee Removal in 1838. Given orders to be humane, he was to remove without appeal the Cherokees who were east of the

Mississippi River. As Cherokee men, women, and children were eating their meals or tending their fields, they were cruelly rounded up by a force of seven thousand (3000 regulars and 4000 citizen soldiers). Soldiers with bayonets tore women from their spinning wheels and children from their toys. Rape, robbery, and murder occurred as this massive force overwhelmed farm after farm, village after village. The citizen soldiers were the most vindictive and cruel. They were followed by white plunderers who confiscated Cherokee possessions and burned Cherokee homes, businesses, and schools. The proud Cherokee people were rounded up into camps, herded as prisoners into pens surrounded by huge stakes and fence posts.

The forced removal in 1838–1839 to lands west of the Mississippi River has been remembered by the Cherokees as "The Trail Where They Cried." Historians have referred to it as the "Trail of Tears." Starvation, disease, cold, and death followed the bloody footsteps of the women, children, and men as they were forcibly marched to the Oklahoma territory. Close to four thousand of the 15,000 Cherokee died on this journey. Evan Jones, an independent Baptist minister who had taught in a mission school in eastern Tennessee since the 1820s and rode a preaching and teaching circuit among the Cherokee people, insisted on moving west with the tribe as well. He had worked with other missionaries to defend tribal homelands, but when extensive efforts with government officials failed, Rev. Jones chose to suffer with his congregants on the Trail of Tears. Surviving the ordeal, Rev. Evan Jones continued to minister among the Cherokee Nation in Oklahoma. He would witness further injustice from the Jackson Administration. For example, the Cherokee people were charged 6 million dollars for the U.S. Government's expense during the removal—in spite of their torturous ordeal and loss of thousands of family members. The United States Government glibly deducted 6 million dollars from the 9 million it had appropriated to "reimburse" the tribe for its vast eastern lands.

As the first half of the nineteenth century drew to a close, the United States Army had pushed all Native Americans away from the main migration routes of white settlers in the east. Most Native Americans who remained alive were now west of the Mississippi River, earlier treaties and assurances by the United States only faint reminders of hopeful negotiations. Part of the Cherokee history was the promise of Article 12 in their agreement with Congress signed in 1785 (before the U.S. Constitution). In this agreement the U.S. Congress stated

> That the Indians may have full confidence in the justice of the United States, respecting their interests, they shall have the right to send a deputy of their choice, whenever they think fit, to Congress.

The War Department could report in 1849 that the Indian frontier was quieter than it had been for five decades. Although the Indian Removal Act of 1830 (as well as President Jackson) had promised that Indian lands west of the Mississippi River were "forever protected" and "forever guaranteed," these legally binding arrangements would be ignored and trampled upon as well. Promises to Native Americans west of the Mississippi River would soon fall (once again) to expediency and greed.

▼ Indian Wars

In 1849 the Congress officially transferred the Bureau of Indian Affairs from the War Department to the newly created Department of the Interior. And yet, except for the period of the Civil War (1861–1865), the United States Army received its main orders and predominant duty for the next four decades in regard to the conflicts between Whites and Native Americans west of the Mississippi River. A line of forts were established along trails and borders. War between the United States and Mexico (1845–1848), the annexation of Texas (1845), the Gadsden Purchase in the Southwest (1853), and the settlement with Britain over the Oregon Country in the Northwest (1846) added tens of thousands of Native Americans under U.S. jurisdiction. The discovery of gold in California in 1849 brought hoards of white prospectors and settlers west, adding to the plight of the Native American inhabitants. California became the thirty-first state on September 9, 1850.

The new "Indian Country" in western lands bordering the Mississippi River began to be invaded by white settlers as well. This area had been labeled "the Great American Desert," and was generally thought to be unfit for agriculture and white settlement. That is why in 1825 Secretary of War John C. Calhoun had recommended it as a "permanent" Indian Country for the eastern tribes. But with the addition of territories further west, the Indian Country no longer defined the border of the United States. It became a thoroughfare between the western and eastern sections of the nation. There was pressure in Congress to divide the "permanent" Indian Country into northern and southern colonies, placing a "corridor to the West" in between.

Gold rushes increased the traffic over the trails that crossed Indian Country, and the railroads would soon transverse the area as well. Indian Commissioner George Manypenny admitted in 1854 that the policy of removal was no longer effective and was entirely unjust. He declared that

> By alternate persuasion and force, some of these tribes have been removed, step by step, from mountains to valley, and

from river to plain, until they have been pushed half-way across the continent. They can go no further.

By 1858 U.S. policy makers asserted that "concentrating the Indians on small reservations of land, and sustaining them there for a limited period until they can be induced to make the necessary exertions to support themselves," was the only alternative to the annihilation of Native Americans. During the 1850s the United States Government garnered an additional 200 million acres of Native American land.

Often conditions agreed upon or forced upon Native Americans by the negotiators were soon violated. For example, in the Treaty of Fort Laramie (1851), the northern Plains tribes granted the right of the United States to establish roads and military posts for annuities. The U.S. Senate, however, shortened the promised timespan of the payments, while carving in boundaries that would later become the states of Kansas (1861), Nebraska (1867), Colorado (1876), North Dakota (1889), South Dakota (1889), Montana (1889), and Wyoming (1890). Black Hawk, a Sioux chief, bluntly told government officials: "You have split the country and I do not like it." The powerful Plains tribes numbered in the hundreds of thousands. North and South, Native Americans attempted to fight the injustices, and a number of chiefs and warriors prepared to do battle. By the end of the 1850s both the Secretary of War and the Secretary of Interior agreed that the Bureau of Indian Affairs should be moved back to the War Department. Only the intervention of the Civil War prevented this action.

During the Civil War soldiers posted to protect the dwindling borders of Native American land were commanded to return to the East to fight. They were replaced by local state volunteers who were even more bigoted and unsympathetic to Native Americans. A number of tribes rebelled at the cru-

elty of the militias and the corruption and incompetence of
the Indian agents. A Sioux uprising occurred in Minnesota
in 1862; Apaches and Navajos fought military units in the
Southwest in the early 1860s. The treachery of white settlers
was incredible. In Arizona, settlers feigned a peace confer-
ence and poisoned twenty-four Apaches who came to talk.
In Colorado, volunteers slaughtered 200 Cheyenne (most of
them women and children) in the Sand Creek Massacre of
1864. The Plains tribes rebelled. By the midpoint of the Civil
War, the United States had sanctioned many more volunteer
troops in the western "Indian Country" than there had been
regular troops in 1860.

Some Native American tribes chose to support either the
North or the South during the Civil War. The Confederacy
promised Native Americans the return of tribal lands if they
fought for the South. The Cherokee warrior, Stand Watie,
became a Brigadier-General in the Confederate Army, taking command of two regiments of Cherokee soldiers in the
Southwest. Union regiments used southern Plains warriors as
scouts. Both North and South garnered soldiers from the remnants of the Five Civilized Tribes, severely punishing those
who chose to fight for the opposition.

A few weeks after the War, the Five Civilized Tribes were
told that they had to give up more of their tribal lands to make
room for other displaced Native Americans. Native Americans throughout the Plains were told bluntly that they must
make room for the onslaught of white settlers. Rebellions were
swiftly crushed. Military posts were strengthened. Trails that
criss-crossed the West were protected. Reservations became
the rule of thumb. Most government officials in the east felt
that it was cheaper to feed Native Americans than to fight
them. Unfortunately, even those friendly to Native Americans believed that tribal culture must be replaced with White
Culture or Native Americans would be exterminated. Every

effort was made to force Native Americans to adopt white ways.

Dissolving the sovereignty of the tribes, a reservation system was planned by the U.S. Government and executed by the U.S. Army. Extermination became a significant military policy toward Native American intransigence and opposition. For example, when Red Cloud's Sioux effectively routed and defeated U.S. soldiers in December 1866, wiping out an entire detachment of eighty men, Lieutenant General Sherman angrily declared: "We must act with vindictive earnestness against the Sioux, even to their extermination, men, women and children." In 1868 General Grant, who continued as the Commanding General of the Army after the Civil War and before his presidency, insisted that he would protect the infiltration of white settlers "even if the extermination of every Indian tribe was necessary to secure such a result." Later in 1868 General Sherman would add: "The more we can kill this year, the less will have to be killed the next war, for the more I see of these Indians the more convinced I am that they all have to be killed or maintained as a species of paupers. Their attempts at civilization are simply ridiculous."

Although the fourteenth Amendment to the Constitution (1868) provided that African-Americans were to have equal national citizenship with whites, Native Americans were denied the vote (and citizenship) in a clause that read, "excluding Indians not taxed." Thus another federal loophole had effectively disenfranchised tribal men. Native Americans were not granted American citizenship until June 2, 1924, when an Act of Congress stipulated that "all non-citizen Indians born within the territorial limits of the United States be, and are hereby declared to be, citizens of the United States."

By the 1880s, reservations overshadowed the United States Army as the principal method of control exercised over the

Native American tribal communities. Complete assimilation, through education and through a bombardment of United States cultural programs, was once again a prominent goal of both reformers and politicians. For example, Lost Bird, the Native American woman whom we introduced at the beginning of this chapter, was not allowed to learn her Sioux language. Nearly four years before her birth the United States government had passed a law forbidding the use of any Native American language. Concerning education, the fiftieth Congress on December 14, 1886, declared that "no books in any Indian language must be used or instruction given in that language," and insisted that "the rule will be strictly enforced."

On October 30, 1990, President George Bush signed into law the Native American Language Act, formally reversing the 104-year-old federal policy of destruction of these languages (and, the accompanying attempted destruction of Native American culture). The one-hundred-and-first Congress stipulated eight provisions of a new United States policy, including the declaration to "preserve, protect and promote the rights and freedom of Native Americans to use, practice, and develop Native American languages." For many, the law was long overdue. That Native Americans and their supporters had to labor for years to get the law passed, and had to amend the bill at the last minute to get it passed before the end of the 101st Congress, underscores the difficulty in righting ancient wrongs.

▲▼▲ 4 ▲▼▲

REGROUPING:
A PERIOD OF TRANSITION

George Hunt Pendleton, senator of Ohio in the 1880s argued on behalf of the General Allotment Act (Dawes Act) that would divide Indian reservations into individual holdings, allowing the rest of the reservation to be sold to white settlers. "They must either change their mode of life or they must die." Later noting that Native American modes of life would change *if* new policies were initiated; the Senator continued, "We may regret it, we may wish it were otherwise, our sentiments of humanity may be shocked by the alternative, but we cannot shut our eyes to the fact that that is the alternative, and that these Indians must either change their modes of life or they will be exterminated." Pendleton explained that

> We must stimulate within them to the very largest degree, the idea of home, of family, and of property. These are the very anchorages of civilization; the commencement of the dawning of these ideas in the mind is the commencement of the civilization of any race, and these Indians are no exception.

That this Democratic sponsor of the Pendleton Act, which created the Civil Service system in 1883, could state such racist pronouncements without regard to Native American views of home, family, property, and civilization seems unbelievable. That so many legislators would agree with him was unconscionable.

Ironically, from 1885 to his death in 1889, George Hunt Pendleton served as United States minister to Germany. In light of his speech this was fitting, because anti-Semites in Germany were making similar statements at that time about Jewish people—statements that would lead to the rise of Adolf Hitler, the Nazi Party, and the murder in concentration camps of approximately six million Jews and five million Gentiles. In America, because of Senator Pendleton and hundreds of other government officials, Native American communities would be further devastated by the policies of the Dawes Act of 1887.

This General Allotment Act enabled the President of the United States to divide a tribe's reservation land into individual parcels for each Native American man, woman, and child. The President was then authorized to declare the "surplus" land to be under the jurisdiction of the United States of America, soon selling it to white homesteaders at $2.50 an acre. Between 1887 and 1930, two-thirds of the remaining Native American land holdings were confiscated by the government through the devices legislated in the Dawes Act. Native Americans lost approximately 90 million acres of land. In every case where this allotment was enacted, the tribes objected to the government's treachery. In many cases the United States had to ignore previous treaty agreements where the government promised to protect the tribe's rights to the land. With a final stab to the heart, the government required Native American communities to pay the costs of surveying and dividing the lands that were being stolen from them. On the Plains, the Sioux uprising in 1890 that ended in the massacre at Wounded Knee Creek was a final desperate attempt among Native Americans to roam the Plains with the freedom and dignity of years past. In the Southwest the Apache fought against both Mexican and U.S troops in a desperate bid for liberty.

▼ The Fight for Freedom

The Apache medicine man, Geronimo, took to the warpath in 1861, the same year the Civil War began. Approaching forty years of age, Geronimo was infuriated that the U.S. Army had captured the great Apache chief Cochise and had hanged his adult male relatives. Geronimo declared that the Native American would no longer be "friendly" with the white man.

An excellent marksman and a visionary with leadership qualities, Geronimo became famous for holding out against both U.S. and Mexican forces for the next twenty-five years. Fearless in battle, he used visions to bolster his remarkable instincts. The Army was only able to decimate his Chiricahua Apache bands by enlisting other antagonistic Apaches to help hunt them down. By 1886 when he surrendered for the final time, nearly 5,000 U.S. Army troops and approximately 3,000 Mexican troops were arrayed against his small band of warriors.

Originally named Goyahka by his family when he was born at the headwaters of the Gila River around the year 1823, the Apache leader received the name Geronimo from the Mexicans when he battled through a hail of their bullets and killed dozens of soldiers with his knife. As the story goes, "Geronimo" refers to "St. Jerome," a patron saint to which the Mexicans pled for help. As the Apache seer and leader would approach the Catholic soldiers, they would cry out, "Geronimo!" The name stuck, and the intransigent Apache became known throughout the United States and Mexico.

Certainly Geronimo hated the Mexicans, attacking without hesitation from the early 1850s. This was because at mid-century a roving band of Mexican soldiers had murdered his mother, young wife, and three children. Twenty other Native American women and children were also massacred in this raid, and the Mexican soldiers sold more than fifty others into slavery. As he burned his family's possessions, including his children's toys, in a break with the past, Geronimo's life became consumed with mystical experiences. On one occasion, a voice called his name four times and then declared:

> No gun can ever kill you. I will take the bullets from the guns of the Mexicans, so they will have nothing but powder. And I will guide your arrows.

With the mistreatment of the great chief Cochise and other Apaches in 1861 by the ill-tempered West Point graduate, Lieutenant George Bascom, Geronimo believed that the "White Eyes," Mexican or American, were to be lifelong enemies. Geronimo and his bands killed thousands in their struggle for survival and their battle for Arizona lands.

Finally imprisoned for the fourth and last time in his early sixties on September 4, 1886, Geronimo and his small band of warriors, women, and children spent the next thirty years as prisoners of war in Florida, Alabama, and Oklahoma. At last Geronimo and his followers were forced to stay at Fort Sill, Oklahoma. In 1909 at the age of eighty-five, he fell off his horse and spent the winter night in a cold ditch. He died of pneumonia four days later. It is said that on his lips at death were the whispered names of his gallant warriors.

In 1905 President Theodore Roosevelt refused Geronimo's request to return to Arizona with his family and tribe, but over half of the tribe was permitted to travel to the Mescalero Reservation in New Mexico four years after his death. "It is my land, my home, my father's land," Geronimo had written Teddy Roosevelt, explaining that he could then "die in peace, feeling that my people, placed in their native homes, would increase in numbers, rather than diminish as at present." The grave of Geronimo is surrounded by hundreds of white headstones in the Apache cemetary at Fort Sill, remnants of his followers. Each stone is engraved with an impersonal number.

▼ The Battle for the Plains

The man who tricked Geronimo into surrendering in 1886 for the sake of his people and with the promise of a reservation in Arizona was General Nelson A. Miles (1839–1925). General Miles asked Lieutenant Charles B. Gatewood, an old acquaintance of Geronimo, to convince the wily Apache leader of Miles' sincerity. Years later, Geronimo met Miles once again and asked him pointedly why he had lied. Miles avoided the question. General Miles, who had ambitions to be President of the United States, even sent his predecessor's faithful Apache scouts to Florida.

On the Plains the Sioux knew all about the vain, ambitious, and deceptive Nelson Miles. The former Boston crockery salesman began his military career as a Civil War volunteer. As a postwar colonel in 1874, Miles led the Fifth Infantry against the Cheyenne at the mouth of Palo Duro Canyon and later campaigned in 1876–1877 against the Sioux. Under pressure from Colonel Miles, Sitting Bull led his people to refuge in Canada for four years. Thirteen years later, as a general in 1890, Miles sent troops to the Pine Ridge and Rosebud Reservations five weeks before the Wounded Knee Massacre.

As a colonel in the 1870s, however, Miles was a contemporary of the infamous Colonel George Armstrong Custer. While the Sioux and Cheyenne were unable to contain Colonel Nelson A. Miles's vain and pompous ambition in the

1870s, they did rid the world of Colonel George A. Custer's power-hungry greed.

George Armstrong Custer

George Custer graduated last in his class from the U.S. Military Academy in 1861. This was the same year that Geronimo went on the warpath and that the Civil War began. Twenty-five years of age by the end of the Civil War, Custer had achieved fame and the rank of major general. As the U.S. Army was scaled down to a smaller entity in the post-war years, Custer became lieutenant colonel of the Seventh Cavalry.

The U.S. Army had little regard for Native Americans, and Custer's views of white superiority were in fashion. For example, Captain William Fetterman, who was assigned to the Bozeman Trail, had boasted in 1866 that he could defeat the entire Sioux nation with a single company. He had little regard for Native American strategy, prowess, or mental capability. On December 21st of the same year, he and all eighty of his men were killed in an ambush by Sioux and Cheyenne warriors. One of the young Lakota warriors who helped to lure Captain Fetterman into the trap was named Crazy Horse. Crazy Horse had many visions and mystical experiences. A tradition arose that he could not be killed by gunfire. A decade later, a more experienced Crazy Horse would lead his people against Custer.

In a campaign against the southern Plains tribes in Kansas in 1867, Custer was court-martialed and suspended for a year because it was alleged he had committed grievous offenses, but he returned the next year to conduct campaigns against Black Kettle's Cheyenne. Dividing his forces in a maneuver of surprise, Custer attacked a Cheyenne village on the Washita River at dawn. He killed over one hundred people, many of them women and children. This atrocity on the early morning of November 27, 1868, however, only increased his fame as an "indian fighter."

In fact, George Custer was a genius of self-promotion, and he became the darling of eastern high society. He used his post on the plains in a quest for riches and to promote business schemes. New York businessmen and society people readily bought shares in his mining and business ventures. The press loved him because he was very accessible and made good copy. The newspapers and magazines portrayed him as a brave and daring indian fighter who risked his life daily, and with blond hair waving in the wind, led his troops into dangerous battle. In reality, he was overbearing and arrogant, rarely taking into consideration the condition of his men. When he felt the press had missed a glorious story about him, he wrote it up himself under a pen name.

From 1873–1876 Colonel Custer and his regiment were headquartered at Fort Abraham Lincoln in the Dakota Territory. In 1873 he helped escort the Northern Pacific Railroad survey, fighting the Sioux in at least two skirmishes. In 1874, under the guise of a scientific survey expedition, the U.S. government sent Custer's Seventh Cavalry to the forbidden Black Hills. The heart of the Lakota Sioux and Cheyenne territory, the sacred Black Hills were supposed to be off limits to Whites. The tribes viewed this area of prayer and meditation as a foodstore and a place of individual replenishing by the Great Spirit. The hot springs there were a natural sauna and mineral bath.

Colonel Custer's entourage included more than 1,000 men, over 100 wagons, and a score of reporters. President Grant's grown son, Frederick, tagged along as well. Most reports acknowledged that Frederick Grant remained drunk most of the journey. The rest of the entourage, including the leader Custer, acted as though they were on a picnic. Sadly, George Custer and his expedition found gold in the sacred Black Hills.

What Native Americans had viewed as a sparkling thing of beauty, Whites clamored to greedily dig up. George Armstrong Custer was front page news once again.

Within a year, 11,000 prospectors moved into the Black Hills. By 1876, over 25,000 were mining and providing services for prospectors. The Sioux called the intruders "thieves" and the government agents "liars," but tried to stay out of the way of such "gold fever." President Grant determined to buy the Black Hills, but to no avail. Sitting Bull's band of Hunkpapa of the Lakota Sioux refused not only to sell, but also defied all edicts of the U.S. Government. The Sioux Nation as a whole began to view Sitting Bull as a symbol of resistance. When asked why he never signed a treaty with the United States, Sitting Bull replied: "What treaty has the white man ever made with us that they have kept. Not one!" It was not within Sitting Bull to compromise any part of the land, lifestyle, or freedom of Native Americans. As a cultural and religious leader, the visionary Sitting Bull had refused to join some chiefs in accepting the Sioux Reservation in 1868. Now the U.S. planned to cut the Black Hills from that "irrevocable treaty."

In the meantime, more and more tribes began to have visions that the "White Eyes" were coming across a great body of water. Indeed, a mass of immigrants from Europe was being lured to the west with the promise of gold, land, and opportunity. Railroads ran great promotion campaigns. Few of these mentioned that a people, the Native Americans, were already on this land. The Lakota Sioux alone had upwards of 50,000 men, women, and children. Soon, the intruding settlers and prospectors would outnumber them four to one. Whereas Native Americans saw forests of game and berries, the white entrepreneurs saw lumber. Whereas Native Americans saw lush meadows and river valleys, the white intruders saw fields of crops. Whereas Native Americans saw the Black Hills as a sacred and serene beauty, the white prospectors saw only gold. Whereas the Native Americans saw a vast homeland to be honored and protected, the white settlers saw an empty land that had no people.

President Ulysses S. Grant and his general Philip H. Sheridan, who headed the Military Division of the Missouri and commanded the large-scale operations against the western tribes in the 1870s, decided that they must end the "Indian Problem" once and for all. An angry September 1875 report of failure by federal commissioners to get the Sioux to open up their land to the whites precipitated the inevitable. The Commissioner of Indian Affairs ordered in November 1875 that all Indians must return to their reservations by January 31, 1876. It is unclear whether or not he realized that this winter period was the most difficult time to travel. He should have realized, however, that the bands of Sioux peoples were still within their treaty parameters. At any rate, General Sheridan planned a three-prong "punitive expedition," converging on the Sioux from the east, south, and west. Ironically, large numbers of Lakota on the reservation began traveling during the spring toward the encampment of Sitting Bull and Crazy Horse. Other bands joined the trek as well. Sitting Bull received a vision of U.S. soldiers falling in their camp.

It was in this atmosphere that the Battle of Grassy Grass (or the Battle of Little Big Horn) occurred. As the forces began to converge on the Cheyenne and Sioux encampments ten days earlier, Crazy Horse of the Oglala Sioux led over a thousand warriors to the south to meet General George Crook's forces at Rosebud. While Sitting Bull prayed in the camp, Crook's armed forces were defeated and repelled by Crazy Horse's forces in the Battle of Rosebud. Unaware of Crook's defeat, the eastern and western columns continued to advance. Custer and his Seventh Cavalry were sent ahead to locate the encampment of Sitting Bull and Crazy Horse and to wait for reinforcements. The last words of Custer's commander were, "Now Custer, don't be greedy. Leave some for us." But George Custer could almost taste more glory and fame. He had written earlier of this effort that he thought "the 7th Cavalry may have its greatest campaign," and booked a speaking tour in anticipation of his triumphant return to the east. In his frenzy to be the first to attack, he drove his weary troops well past midnight.

Although his Crow scouts warned him that he was approaching a massive encampment, he did not respect their caution in the midst of potential glory. Custer divided his forces for a surprise attack, just as he had massacred the Cheyenne villagers on the Washita River seven years before. The thought of more screaming women and children did not bother him. The element of surprise could mean victory. When his Native American scouts began putting on their tribal garb in preparation for death, again warning him that they would all die, Custer discharged the scouts. This, ironically, saved the scouts' lives. Crazy Horse repelled the early attacks by Custer's division commanders and was surprised to find Custer charging into one of the thickest areas of warriors.

By Native American accounts (the only living witnesses), there was no "Last Stand of Custer":—he died early in the battle. Furthermore, the battle lasted only twenty minutes. Those under George Custer's immediate command were all killed as a deluge of arrows and warriors fell upon them. Neither was Custer "ringed by dead Sioux." His publicity machine just continued to manufacture stories even after his death! Reporters hundreds of miles from the Battle of Little Big Horn turned it into a heroic martyrdom and a gallant "last stand." They described Custer's flowing "yellow hair" once again, and pictured their hero falling last of all, surrounded by thousands of indians. It made good copy to sell more newspapers and magazines to eastern whites. No journalist thought about the Native Americans protecting their women and children in the three-mile-long encampment. No reporter envisioned the screams of women and children faced with armament and guns.

Sitting Bull, who was too old to be in the battle with the young warriors and who was a holy man not a chief, was portrayed in the press as the culprit. Demeaning racism toward Native Americans and religious prejudice toward Catholics came together in the reports that French Jesuits had taught Sitting Bull Napoleonic war strategy. Related rumors persisted for years that Sitting Bull was actually a white man, expelled from West Point as a student! Tracked down in Canada by East Coast reporters, Sitting Bull declared: "They say I murdered Custer. It is a lie. He was a fool and rode to his death." In plays and "Wild West" shows Custer died his mythical death thousands of times a year.

The Native Americans, true to their nature and belief, did not amass for one final kill against U.S. troops, but rather split up into bands and left the area. They just wanted to be left alone. The Custer publicity, however, led more individuals to cry out for the extermination of those "indians" who would not "return to the reservation." With a seemingly popular mandate, the U.S. Army mobilized its entire western force against the Sioux and Cheyenne. As troops burned Native American villages and supplies, small band after small band began to surrender. The same month Sitting Bull entered Canada, Crazy Horse led 300 starving families into the Red Cloud Agency to surrender. Convinced that he would continue to be a troublemaker, the Army conjured up a reason to imprison him. When he tried to escape, Crazy Horse was bayoneted in the back. He died that night. His loyal followers whisked his body away and secretly buried it. They then took a blood-oath never to reveal where he was buried.

The freedom loving Sioux found reservation life demoralizing and unbearable. George Armstrong Custer had revelled in the tide of immigration to the Plains, insisting that hundreds of thousands of settlers were "enlarging the limits of civilization." For the Native American, however, much was being destroyed. Millions of buffalo were killed, wiping out the source of food for the Plains tribes. Railroads crisscrossed the continent. Sitting Bull had to return his starving people to the United States and was promptly incarcerated on the reservation. After a decade the revival of the Ghost Dance Religion encouraged Native Americans once again. Through traditional dancing it was believed that the Great Spirit would return, and would bring back the wildlife and the buffalo. The Great Spirit would force the "White Eyes" to leave once and for all. It was this revival of dancing and religious fervor that led to a final gasp for freedom and the old way of life.

The Indian Agent of the Standing Rock Reservation, James McLaughlin, was fearful of the Ghost Dance Religion. He and Sitting Bull had never seen eye to eye. Sitting Bull was a tough negotiator, and when it had appeared in 1887 that government officials wanted more land, Sitting Bull took a handful of dirt and slowly let it spill to the ground. "I won't sell even this much dirt," he declared defiantly. Just as defiantly, he refused to stifle the Ghost Dance Religion. Sitting Bull would die during McLaughlin's attempt to defuse the religous fervor, and the following Wounded Knee Massacre would occur as federal troops were called in. The memory of women and children cut apart by artillery in the snow-covered field of Wounded Knee in 1890 would never be forgotten. Decades later an eyewitness, Black Elk, holy man of the Oglala Sioux, wrote:

And so it was over. I did not know then how much was ended. When I look back now from this high hill of my old age, I can still see the butchered women and children lying heaped and scattered all along the crooked gulch as plain as when I saw them with eyes still young. And I can see that something else died there in the bloody mud, and was buried in the blizzard. A people's dream died there. It was a beautiful dream.

This devastation of Native Americans was not enough for an expanding United States. During the same period white settlers clamored for more land and the U.S. Congress obliged their electorate once again at Native American expense. In 1891 Congress amended the General Allotment Act to allow ranchers, farmers, and miners to lease tribal lands. Settlers invaded the territory in larger numbers. Congress established the Dawes Commission in 1893 to renegotiate existing treaty agreements. When Native Americans balked at the Commission's proposals for additional allotments, Congress passed the Curtis Act of 1898. This Act dissolved tribal governments and initiated the allotments the government wanted. Ironically, the Curtis Act was entitled "an Act for the protection of the people of the Indian Territory, and for other purposes."

Under such duress and repressive measures, Native Americans had to regroup in the next century in a resilient effort to survive. The United States government, in turn, was convinced to turn once again to education and acculturalization to meld Native Americans into the American mainstream. Educators began with the Native Americans' most precious legacy: their children.

▼ The Boarding School Movement

The Civil War interrupted the formal education that Indian rights advocates had set in place during the antebellum period. After the war, numbers of societies and individuals sought to restore and expand the original efforts. From government officials in the Bureau of Indian Affairs to missionaries and social workers, they sought to "induce" Native American children to attend school. In 1870 Congress authorized 100,000 dollars a year for schooling these children, building schools and paying teachers with government funds. By 1883 this appropriation had jumped to 2.3 million dollars. While more than half of this appropriation funded schools on the reservation (most of them elementary day schools), the rest of the appropriation became earmarked for off-reservation boarding schools. The first of these nonreservation government boarding schools was the Carlisle Indian Industrial School founded in Carlisle, Pennsylvania, in 1879.

Richard Henry Pratt (1840–1924) founded the Carlisle Indian Industrial School in the hope of accomplishing with Native American young people the educational success he felt he had had with tribal prisoners of war. A seasoned career Army officer and veteran of the Civil War, Lieutenant Pratt had close contact with Native Americans as he led Indian scouts on the frontier. Watching young warriors shackled in an ice house on the grounds of Fort Sill, Oklahoma, Pratt volunteered to take charge of the Native American prisoners of war. Working with them day by day, he believed that they were also shackled mentally and spiritually by an outmoded way of life. He wrote to General Sheridan that reform of these young prisoners should be attempted while they were incarcerated. The U.S. Government concurred and Lt. Pratt was put in charge of an educational experiment.

Still shackled, the prisoners were moved 1200 miles east to Fort Marion, an old Spanish fort in St. Augustine, Florida, that had been turned into a military prison. Pratt had their chains removed, bathed them, cut their hair, and replaced their tribal clothing with U.S. Army uniforms. It was Pratt's belief that there was nothing worth preserving in Native American culture. The only hope for the tribes was to divest themselves of their antiquated beliefs and practices and to imitate as closely as possible the culture of White Anglo-Saxon Protestantism. The "savage" must be "raised" to the level of civilized society. Pratt recruited local volunteers to teach English to the warriors. When one of the most trusted of his prisoner/students plotted with two others to escape, Pratt secretly gave them a sleeping potion and had them carted out of the complex as though they were dead. The other prisoners watched the "wagon of death" leave the complex, but they also watched as the wagon returned with the three now awakened warriors. The appearance was as Pratt wanted. It proved to the prisoners that Pratt was a powerful medicine man, and he was able to develop crucial mind control over the Native American prisoners.

It must be noted that Richard Henry Pratt's concepts and ideals were among the most lofty of his day. These concepts of civilization were the bulwark of the humanitarian and missionary enterprises of the latter nineteenth century. The concept of "Americanizing" the uncivilized masses was practiced toward European immigrants as well. Ministers, educators, social workers, and philanthropists defended such beliefs. It was the prevalent mindset of those who truly cared for others. Unlike the racists of the day, Pratt and his humanitarian colleagues did believe that Native Americans were human beings.

And yet, they bought into the same pseudosciences of the day that would give rise to twentieth-century fascist movements. Like anti-Semitic Germans who emphasized the "science" of physiognomy (the art of judging character by physical features), the Smithsonian sent a sculptor to make face masks of Pratt's prisoner/students. It was "scientifically" judged from these face masks that indians were self-reliant, but were for the most part destructive, secretive, and drawn toward strong drink. When word of "Custer's Last Stand" reached the good people of St. Augustine who had employed and taught Pratt's students, they fearfully asked him to lock the "savages" up at night. Pratt reminded the hysterical citizens that his students had recently been up past two A.M. helping the people of St. Augustine fight a dangerous and ravaging fire.

When his students were released by government edict in 1878, Pratt arranged for seventeen of his students to enter the only school that would accept them: the Hampton Normal and Agricultural School in Hampton, Virginia. This private institution was founded to educate black students in industrial skills to help them survive in the modern world. Pratt believed that his student's education had just begun and that the industrial boarding school was the key to Indian education. The federal government paid a fee for each Native American student Pratt enrolled, and Pratt traveled to the eastern cities to garner additional funds. A group of Christian reformers called "Friends of the Indian" sent considerable help. They saw as providential Pratt's ambition to civilize the savage. In turn, Pratt broadened his educational crusade. He told the Secretary of State that if he would give him 300 young indians and a school in one of the best communities, Pratt would show him how to solve the Indian Problem. Pratt was not only given permission to recruit the reservation children, but also was given a former military training post in Carlisle, Pennsylvania. And so, the Carlisle Indian Industrial School, the model for the movement, was born in 1879.

As a career military man, Richard Henry Pratt believed that Indian education should combine military regimen with hard work and stringent cultural immersion. Every moment of every day was planned for the students. With military discipline they awoke by bugles and ate at stages by bells. Rebellious students were punished in dank cells and whipped. The young student's hair was cut, uniforms were issued, shoes replaced mocassins, and all vestiges of Native American culture were eradicated. Only English was to be spoken, and the student had to choose an English name from a board of names. The goal was to impart the value system of an emerging industrial society, that is, hard work, ambition, goal-orientatedness, and a willingness to stand alone as an individual. Native American culture, which emphasized responsibility to the group, was to be severed from the child's orientation. "Americanization" meant taking care of yourself and rising to be the best that you could be. The Carlisle School taught reading, writing, and arithmetic for half of the school day, and taught farming and trades the other half. For men, "trades" meant carpentry, harness-making, tinsmithing, printing, masonry, machine-tending, and so on. For women, trade meant cooking, washing, sewing, dressmaking, nursing, ironing.

The key was separating the child from tribal life. The child was not allowed to visit the reservation. The occasional visits from family were regulated and monitored. Even so, Pratt soon realized that as long as the reservation existed, he could not totally eradicate the culture. "The end to be gained is the complete civilization of the Indian," Pratt counseled in a letter to Massachusetts Senator Henry L. Dawes (the senator after whom the Dawes Commission was named), concluding that "the sooner all tribal relations are broken up; the sooner the Indian loses all his Indian ways, even his language, the better it will be." Like the federal government, Pratt had hoped that reservations would be broken into individual farms and that the Native American would be totally assimilated into the great "melting pot" of America. He bitterly opposed the existence of reservations and Native American culture his whole life.

After an initial year of struggle over shortages of food, clothing, medicine, and willing teachers, Pratt's school blossomed. The school program increased from three to five years and, within a decade, it had over 1,000 Native American children and teenagers from reservations across the United States. On the West Coast, Forest Grove opened as a boarding school in Oregon in 1880, followed by more institutions such as Genoa in Nebraska and Haskell in Kansas in 1884. By the turn of the century there were twenty-five off-reservation boarding schools located in thirteen states. The establishment of the earlier schools was largely funded by the government sale of Osage tribal lands in Kansas for 500,000 dollars. But soon Congress was questioning paying 150 dollars per year for boarding schools, as well as additional expenses in transportation, compared to 30 dollars per year for a day school on the reservation. Salaries for immigrant workers during this period only approximated 500 dollars a year. By 1886, Congressional restrictions were put on the amount of money that could be spent to build additional schools. Congress believed that the churches should take a more active role in Indian education, but at the same time fought with the missionaries over the use of Native American languages in preaching the Gospel on the reservations and in the schools.

While Richard Henry Pratt drummed up financial support from charities to supplement government funding, it was becoming more apparent that there had been problems in his school and in others from the beginning. Some students never even played the game of adapting to white culture and were openly hostile. Broken hearts and loneliness contributed to scores of deaths among the children, and the graveyard of the Carlisle Indian Industrial School had many white tombstones with the engraved English names of Native American children. Furthermore, Pratt's "outing system" of housing Native American students with white families during breaks and vacation periods underscored the deep resentments and prejudices. Many families treated the students as educated servants. Unfortunately, even the most assimilated and competent at graduation found a similar prejudice among employ-ers. Many ended up back on the reservation, never to be heard from again. Sadly, the children in Pratt's boarding school, like his former prisoners, were the victims of the good intentions of white humanitarianism. Richard Henry Pratt retired as superintendent of the Carlisle Indian Industrial School in 1904. He died in 1924, just two months before Native Amer-icans were granted American citizenship. On June 2, 1924, the Indian Citizenship Act was passed, making all nonciti-zen Native Americans born in the United States citizens. The Supreme Court had determined, however, that the granting of citizenship did not terminate federal responsibility for Native Americans.

▼ The Indian New Deal

Even before the end of the First World War, it became apparent that government policy as well as misguided reform movements had devastated Native American families and communities. A dwindled Native American population of approximately 250,000 was dwarfed in a nation approaching 100 million. Programs to make the Native American into a property-owning farmer and to desolve tribal affiliations led to hunger, disease, exploitation, and despair. Most of the acts passed by Congress in the first two decades of the twentieth century culminated in the transfer of millions of acres more of Native American land to white ownership.

In an effort to soften the blatant efforts of some states to infringe on reservation rights, Congress sought to increase federal jurisdiction and to give more power to the Secretary of Interior and the Commissioner of Indian Affairs. Unfor-tunately, the men who held these posts (while sympathetic in speeches toward the plight of the Native Americans) focused their energies on forcing Native Americans to assimilate to white culture and to forsake their own tribal culture. Reports on the spread of tuberculosis and trachoma in the wretched squalor of the reservations led to an increase in Congressional appropriations toward health care for Native Americans, but also fueled the call for assimilation. Though these periodic appropriations in the early decades of the twentieth century fell far short of the actual medical needs of Native Americans, impatient calls to limit federal guardianship over reservations increased. As always, more attention was given to Native American property than to the Native American people.

John Collier and the American Indian Defense Association

John Collier (1884–1968) was a reformer who had worked in New York City among the teeming millions of immigrants during the early decades of the twentieth century. He had labored fervently to create neighborhood community organizations that would take decision-making responsibility for the political, economic, social, religious, and cultural affairs of each ward. The First World War convinced Collier that western civilization was bent upon destroying itself and that the American emphasis upon individualism and materialism could destroy the rest of the world.

In 1919 John Collier moved to California to work among migrant workers and western immigrants for the State of California. Losing this position during the "Red Scare" in 1920, Collier learned of the Pueblo culture in New Mexico. The Native American worldview of the Pueblos impressed Collier as being far superior to the dominant American concepts, and he determined to save Pueblo society. In 1923 he organized the American Indian Defense Association in an effort to defend Native Americans against the assimilationist philosophy initiated in the provisions of the Dawes Severalty

Act of 1887 (and subsequent legislation and government action). Under Executive Secretary Collier's direction and supported by a small group of liberally-oriented individuals from California, the American Indian Defense Association successfully defended Native American title to remaining reservation lands and alerted the public to the unfair treatment Native Americans had endured (and were enduring). The American Indian Defense Association forced the government to remove a number of restrictions on Native American culture and the practice of tribal religious ceremonies.

Throughout the 1920s the American Indian Defense Association worked diligently to uphold the Native American right to basic civil liberties, public health services, agricultural advice and assistance, and communal and corporate enterprise. Collier helped Native Americans in their quest to organize effectively, and he fought against the boarding school movement. Such pressure for reform and credible information led the Brookings Institution to strongly condemn federal policy under the Dawes Act and to criticize the Bureau of Indian Affairs for emphasizing Native American property to the detriment of the Native American people. Although commissioned by the Bureau of Indian Affairs, the highly respected Brookings Institution's early 1928 critical findings, *The Problem of Indian Administration* (popularly referred to as the Meriam Report), uncovered a federal policy that had ravaged the Native American people through greed, avarice, boarding schools, confiscation of property, legal technicalities, and neglect.

This Meriam Report called for more appropriations toward reservation educational and health programs, and suggested more political and economic autonomy in tribal decision-making. Urging that the federal government change its "point of view," this report encouraged the United States government to adopt a policy of cultural pluralism that would allow a Native American to "live according to his old culture." The 1928 Meriam Report pleasantly surprised John Collier in its candor as much as it shocked the Bureau of Indian Affairs that had hoped for a more positive portrayal of its efforts.

The election of President Herbert Hoover later that year provided an administration that was in sympathy with the humanitarian impulse of the Meriam Report. Hoover's vice president, Charles Curtis (1860–1936), had a mother who was part Kaw in tribal background. In 1929 Hoover replaced a traditional Commissioner of Indian Affairs with fellow Quaker, Charles Rhoads. Rhoads' assistant commissioner, Henry Scattergood, was also a member of the Friends' faith. President Hoover assured them that he would support them in their efforts to implement the recommendations of the Meriam Report. Even the new Secretary of Interior, Ray Lyman Wilbur, wholeheartedly cooperated with them on educational and health care reform as well as on appointing a more qualified personnel in the Bureau of Indian Affairs. Yet none of these men were willing to strengthen tribal political and economic powers. Their belief in individualism prevented them from strengthening tribal cohesion. Native American lands were in danger of further confiscation through allotment.

John Collier spotted this vacillation among Hoover and his appointees and immediately contacted the Senate Indian Affairs Committee. Through his efforts, the senators visited most of the major reservations between 1928 and 1932. Impressed by these on-location visits as well as by Collier's arguments, the senators were convinced that the land-allotment system must be ended and that further reforms were necessary. As the nation slowly dropped into the black hole of the Great Depression, Hoover was soundly defeated in the Election of 1932 by Franklin Delano Roosevelt. The nation appeared to be ready to change federal policy toward Native

Americans in the same way that it was ready to accept innovative economic proposals. John Collier figured heavily in the Roosevelt Administration's plans.

In April 1933, John Collier accepted the position of Commissioner of Indian Affairs in Franklin Delano Roosevelt's new administration. Ironically, the new Secretary of Interior, Harold Ickes, was also a charter member of the American Indian Defense Association. Ickes respected Collier as the most knowledgeable expert on Native Americans and turned to him frequently for advice. John Collier immediately began working to establish total reform. He spent his first months of office working feverishly on legislation to repeal the Dawes Act and to replace thousands of pages of federal legislation with a reorganization act. Collier's original submission to Congress was an act fifty-two pages long. It contained provisions that would increase tribal autonomy and return alloted lands to tribal control. Immediately receiving opposition from Native Americans who did not want their individual allotments returned to tribal control and from Congress who did not want tribes to gain more political and economic control, the Indian Reorganization Act of 1934 was passed as a compromise. It did, however, abolish the allotment system.

Working around Congress through Roosevelt's New Deal agencies to accomplish his original undiluted reforms, John Collier was responsible for many of the changes in Native American affairs in the 1930s and during the Second World War. He fought to enlarge reservations and to revive Native American tribal governments. Through the Public Works Administration Collier obtained jobs for Native Americans. Through the Farm Security Administration he obtained funds to rehabilitate Native American land. Although during his years as commissioner from 1933–1945 he was partially successful in reviving Native American culture in the Southwest, John Collier never could convince Congress that Native

Americans should not be encouraged to forsake their culture. In the Dakotas and Oklahoma the federal government continued to exert immense pressures on Native Americans to abandon their culture and to totally assimilate into white culture. When the Congress in 1944 voted to eliminate the special status of Native Americans and resolved to more blatantly attempt to assimilate them into white society, John Collier could take no more. He resigned his office as Commissioner of Indian Affairs in January of 1945. Secretary of the Interior Harold Ickes resigned a year later.

Postwar Policy

With the resignations of two thirteen-year veterans in such important posts, Congress received control over affairs concerning Native Americans almost by default. Problems abounded. For example, in 1946 it was reported that 75 percent of Navajo children ages 6–18 (an estimated 18,000 young people) were not attending school. The same year Congress created the Indian Claims Commission to settle disputes between Native Americans and the federal government. Some of these disputes stretched back into the nineteenth century. Congress extended the life of the Indian Claims Commission five times until its jurisdiction finally expired on September 30, 1978. Over six hundred claims had been filed by this date, a majority receiving monetary compensation and a relative few receiving land restitution. All claims that had not been settled by this expiration date were transferred to the United States Court of Claims. During the 1970s and early 1980s a relatively few tribes regained possession of former tribal lands through long and hard-fought legal battles. The Indian Claims Limitation Act of 1982 passed by Congress amended the Statute of Limitations for pre-1966 claims. Those pre-1966 claims not registered with the Secretary of Interior by 1982 had little chance of being considered.

While federal policy wavered during the 1950s, Native Americans regrouped during that decade to join the increasing call for civil rights and minority equality. Native Americans fought bravely in the Second World War and worked diligently in the defense industries. Like the African-Americans, they could no longer accept the role of second-class citizens and the brunt of local and state discrimination. The growth and rebirth of Native American organizations blossomed after 1961. These organizations demanded control over programs that affected their communities; they published the plight of their people and battled to receive their fair share of life, liberty, and the pursuit of happiness—their share of the "American Dream." In their critique of American society, student protests of the 1960s and early 1970s encompassed the civil rights and historic treatment of Native Americans as well. Wounded Knee was reoccupied in an armed protest in 1973 (from February 7th to May 8th).

The Supreme Court during the 1960s, 1970s, and 1980s repeatedly affirmed the sovereign powers of Native American tribes. The years between 1965 and 1975 witnessed the passage of the most significant legislation to affect Native American education since the establishment of the republic, culminating in The Indian Self-Determination and Education Assistance Act of 1975. The American Indian Religious Freedom Act of 1978 protected traditional Native American religious practices. A century after the Dawes Severalty Act, the government of the United States of America changed its national policy from a denial of tribal sovereignty to a qualified full recognition of tribal sovereignty and cultural integrity. While self-determination had some pitfalls and federal policy still contained contradictions, a major national policy shift had indeed occurred.

The same year that Richard Henry Pratt founded the
Carlisle Indian Industrial School in Carlisle, Pennsylvania,
Chief Joseph of the Nez Pierce declared the following in a
speech in Washington, D.C.

> We ask only an even chance to live as other men. Let me be
> a free man. Free to work. Free to trade where I choose. Free
> to choose my own teachers. Free to follow the religion of my
> fathers. Free to think and talk and act for myself.

It had taken the American government and many American citizens a whole century to heed his cry and the cry of
his Native American community.

5

▲▼▲　　　　　　　　▲▼▲

RELIGIOUS ENCOUNTERS

n ovember 25, 1992, the State of Georgia formally pardoned two Congregational missionaries who had spent most of their lives working and preaching among the Cherokee. The missionaries, Samuel Austin Worcester and Elihu Butler, had spent 16 months in hard labor on a chain gang because they defended Native American rights, refused to leave their ministries in the Cherokee Nation, and legally opposed the State of Georgia in the 1830s. It took the State of Georgia 160 years to admit that it had usurped Cherokee sovereignty, that it had wrongfully incarcerated the Christian missionaries, that it had ignored the Supreme Court, and that its actions were "a stain on the history of criminal justice in Georgia."

Samuel Austin Worcester was one of the most important missionaries to the Cherokee Nation. By the age of 27 he had dedicated his life to serving the Cherokees and had worked to make the Cherokee syllabary developed by Sequoya suitable for printing. After moving to New Enchota, the capital of the Cherokee Nation in 1827, he helped the Native Americans in their quest to publish a newspaper, and the famed *Cherokee Phoenix* tribal newspaper was published the following year. Worcester believed that the use of Native American language was crucial in understanding their culture and teaching the Christian message to them. In his evangelistic fervor, Samuel Worcester translated the Bible into Cherokee and wrote religious tracts that described the process of salvation. He was highly respected in the Cherokee community.

When gold was found on sovereign Cherokee lands in 1829 the State of Georgia began to confiscate much of the Cherokee Nation and declared that it was officially abolishing Cherokee sovereignty within the State of Georgia. With Andrew Jackson in the White House, Georgians knew they had the support of an anti-Indian president. But Worcester and Butler opposed the state and, with others, drew national attention to the plight of the Cherokee. In an effort to silence the missionaries the State of Georgia enacted a law requiring all white men living on Cherokee land to obtain a state license. The State of Georgia was thus proving that it had jurisdiction over the Cherokee Nation and that it could refuse entry to those who opposed state actions.

Samuel Worcester and Elihu Butler refused, were arrested, and convicted of "high misdemeanor." They were sentenced to four years of hard labor. Worcester and Butler appealed to the United States Supreme Court. In 1832 Chief Justice John Marshall declared that Georgia had no constitutional right to extend any state laws over the Cherokee, could not seize Cherokee land, and that the Cherokee must have the protection of the federal government. "It is difficult to comprehend," Chief Justice Marshall wrote for the court, that those who "discovered" America could be given rights "which annulled the existing right of its ancient possessors." The Supreme Court ruled that the missionaries must be released.

Georgia ignored the ruling of the Supreme Court, and President Andrew Jackson as head of the executive branch of the federal government refused to protect Cherokee rights. Rev. Worcester and Rev. Butler suffered horribly, and were released only in time to join the Cherokee in their forced evacuation to Oklahoma. As we saw in chapter three, President Andrew Jackson not only ignored the Supreme Court, but also mercilessly forced the Cherokee Nation to leave their homeland and move west of the Mississippi River to a new "Indian Territory."

Samuel Austin Worcester survived the horrid trek, spending the rest of his life helping the Cherokee adapt to their Oklahoma reservation. He printed the Bible and an almanac in the Cherokee language, established the Park Hill Mission for the Cherokee, and organized numerous study groups, social services, and clubs for Cherokee of all ages. He died in 1859, a couple of years before the Civil War ravaged the Cherokee domain. Remembering his courage a century-and-a-half later, spokeswoman Marsha Bailey of the State Board of Pardons and Paroles explained on November 22, 1992, that "This is one of many injustices done, but its something that we could do something about." State legislator Bill Dover, whose lineage was part Cherokee, stated that the pardon was a sign that the State of Georgia had finally realized the scope of its mistreatment of Native Americans.

▼ Early Encounters

By the time Europeans arrived in the New World, Native American cultures had gone through many changes and adaptations over the millennia. As we have seen in previous chapters, interaction between Native American tribes was extensive even before white settlement. Some important Native American cultures had declined, while others had disappeared hundreds of years before the explorers landed. Nevertheless, European contact would escalate change and challenge Native American culture as never before.

For all of the varying spiritual orientations and religious adaptations of diverse Native American tribes, there were certain constants in their religion and culture. Native Americans emphasized group identity and asserted that a tribesperson must never acquire wealth and fame at the expense of another. Taking one's place in society, respecting tradition, and maintaining a cooperative spirit were bulwarks of Native American society. The dictums of never taking the land for granted and never being able to consume the land personally were also widely taught. Even the few private ownership groups emphasized the communal aspects of the land and the obligation to live in harmony with the earth. Ever conscious of the group and subordinating themselves to their tribal brothers and sisters, each member of the tribe strove to support and sustain the tribe willingly and selflessly. Dancing was (and is) the key to most religious rituals. To this day the ancient saying among Native Americans prevails: "**We Always Remember Who We Are As Long As We Keep Dancing.**"

So oriented were both the Spanish missionaries in the Southwest and the Pueblo people to ritual that the Pueblos often incorporated Spanish Catholic beliefs and practices into their Native American rituals. The European advantage of offering new plants, animals, tools, and technology initially helped Spanish missionaries to spread their religious message among the Pueblos. The task, however, was too great; the number of laborers was far too small. Few Spanish missionaries took the time to learn about Pueblo culture or to even stay in a tribe long enough to learn its language. Nevertheless, missionaries claimed to have converted nearly 20,000 Pueblo tribespeople by the year 1620 (some reports claimed 35,000 by year 1625).

Under the unbearable domination of Spanish authorities, and with increasing conflict with Spanish soldiers, a diminishing Pueblo village system rebelled in the latter decades of the 1600s. By this time the Pueblo peoples had determined that the Spanish religious system had not brought them better harvests and a better life as promised by Spanish missionaries. Spanish Catholicism increasingly appeared to be a foreign religious system and an inadequate religious philosophy. Of those Pueblos who practice some mode of Hispanic Christianity today, traditional Native American beliefs often relegate the European system to external and peripheral ritualism.

In like manner, in the early decades of the 1600s, French Franciscan missionaries to the Northeastern tribes refused to stay in the Native American villages or learn their customs. They failed in their missionary activity. By 1625, however, a good number of French Jesuits replaced the ineffectual Franciscans and overcame great obstacles by respecting Native American culture and learning Native American language. Some Jesuits even had a favorable opinion of the Northeastern tribal religion and capitalized on the similarities between tribal spirituality and Catholic Christianity. While the Jesuits emphasized personal commitment and the quest for God's guidance, the Northeastern tribes respected supernatural power as well, seeking out spiritual guidance through dreams and visions. Both groups stressed morality and ritual as well as proper worship. In addition, Catholic saints could be compared to Native American guardian spirits.

Although the Jesuits realized the differences of the Native American belief system, they sought to teach the Christian religion by relating it to local religious and social custom. This attitude of building on common denominators to gradually reshape tribal customs was honed to a sharp precision during a century of Jesuit missions around the world. By midcentury, gifts and special privileges were added to the benefits of becoming a "Christian." By 1648, in the midst of disease and decline, one Huron tribesperson in five described his or her belief as "Christian." As the Iroquois warriors began to destroy one Huron town after another some Jesuits chose to die with their converts. In 1650, Native American Christians were invited by the Jesuits to move to the protected Saint Lawrence Valley. Today their descendants have assimilated to European custom and much Native American Huron culture has been lost.

▼ English Missions

When encountering Christian missionaries and their claims, Native Americans often appear to have asked them about the tangible benefits of the Christian faith and the practical effects of such a faith. Whether Catholic or Protestant, Jesuit or Puritan, the missionary had to describe whether or not Christian belief could protect the tribe, provide healing, and prevent poverty and loss. Native Americans wanted to know why they were required to change their rituals and alter their lifestyles. Why was European tradition thought to be superior to proven tribal traditions? Nowhere is the dialogue spelled out so clearly than in the Puritan encounters with the New England tribes. While relatively few Puritan ministers took it upon themselves to minister to Native Americans, and only a handful attempted to learn about Native American culture, a few exemplify the desire to reach their Native American neighbors and to attempt a viable discourse with them. One of these individuals was the Englishman and Puritan minister, John Eliot (1604–1690), often described as the "Apostle to the Indians."

John Eliot

Born in Essex County, England, and educated at Cambridge University, John Eliot arrived in the Massachusetts Bay

Colony in November, 1631. Taking a pastorate near Boston in the town of Roxbury the next year, Rev. Eliot also taught school to make ends meet. He would be the pastor of the Roxbury congregation for more than 57 years.

While there appears to have been criticism from England that the Massachusetts Bay colonists had not attempted adequately to christianize the Native Americans in the area, John Eliot became aware of Native Americans in his region during the Pequot War (1636–1637). Busy with his ministry, he neglected to learn more about the tribes that surrounded him. In 1643, however, Eliot began learning the Massachusett native language and by 1646 was able to preach simple sermons in that Native American language. His first sermon was preached to a group of Native Americans who lived near Dorchester. Hoping to expound upon some elementary biblical truths, Rev. Eliot was caught off guard when the tribal peoples began asking him concrete questions about where thunder and wind come from and why the tides of the sea are so regular. John Eliot was forced to return home for more linguistic study.

In the next 40 years, Rev. John Eliot became progressively more proficient in communicating his theology. Some Native Americans responded favorably, and these converts became known as "Praying Indians." In 1654, Eliot printed an Algonkian translation of the Shorter Catechism and in 1661 published the New Testament for Massachusett converts. In 1663 he finished translating the complete Bible, and in a few short years published a number of simple theological works as well as religious tracts. Eliot's translation of the Bible into a Native American language was the first Bible printed in the Western Hemisphere.

In addition, Rev. John Eliot's *Indian Primer* was used in fledgling Native American schools set up in "praying towns" composed of his converts. By 1674, over 1100 Native Amer-

icans lived in fourteen of these special towns, many only
"potential" Christians. Twenty-four Native Americans were
ordained as Congregational ministers, and others taught in
the schools. Although Puritan attempts to enroll Native
American Christians in New England colleges met with little success, the local schools served as a tool of acculturation.
A small "indian college" was associated with Harvard College, and Joel Hiacoomes and Caleb Cheeshahteaumuck,
Native American products of advanced Puritan grammar
schools, persevered through numerous obstacles and graduated.

Rev. Thomas Mayhew, Jr., established the first Protestant
mission and school for Native Americans on Martha's Vineyard in 1643, and the Mayhew family cared for this mission
school for five generations. Knowledgeable of the Massachusett language and honoring Native American land claims,
Rev. Mayhew employed a personal, respectful, and quiet witness to the Massachusett tribes. Conversions multiplied. A
Native American Christian community was established in
1652 and, after nearly two decades of proving to other Puritans that they were indeed "converted," the first Christian
church with Native American officials was chartered in 1670.
Thousands of Native American Christians lived in towns on
islands surrounding the Mayhew complex, and the witness of
these communities reached into settlements on the main-
land, paralleling the efforts of Eliot.

Hoping to aid the work of future evangelists in the New
World, John Eliot wrote *Indian Dialogues*, first published in
1671. In the dialogues he summarizes various encounters and
discussions with nonconverted Native Americans. As with
so many Puritan ministers, Eliot failed to capitalize on the
similarities between Native American religion and the Christian faith that would have helped him to explain Christian
theology. These Native Americans had a deep consciousness

of spiritual forces active in their daily lives, and they readily accepted the fact that the world was not of their own making. Their Jehovah-like being in the heavens was often described as Manitou. Private prayers as well as community ceremonies were practiced. They were a deeply religious people. Rev. Eliot, however, demeaned their religion and discredited their social values. His goal was to "civilize the savage" as well as to christianize. To Eliot, civilization was equated with the best of Christian English culture.

With a triumphalism that is unbelievable at times from a man who genuinely seemed to care about Native American people, Eliot begins his *Indian Dialogues* by challenging them to "turn from their lewd and lazy life." Converts are said to have called their former life "filth and folly." And yet, Rev. Eliot had to explain the vulgar actions of his fellow countrymen. In one passage, his Christian speaker relates that

> We know there be many sins among the English, which provoke God to be angry with them, and to punish them, to the end he might bring them to repentance. When we exhort you to pray, and to serve the God of the English, we call you to imitate the virtues and good ways of the English, wherein you shall be acceptable to the Lord. We do not call you to imitate their sins, whereby they and you shall provoke the anger and displeasure of the Lord. And what though God doth chastise his people for their sins? It is his wisdom, faithfulness, and love so to do. A child will not run away from his wise and loving father, because he chastises him for his faults, but love him the better, fear him the more, and learn thereby to be a good child. The wise English love God the more, for his wise chastisement of them for their sins. And why may not I use it as an argument to persuade you to choose him to be your God, who will love and encourage you in all virtue, and love and punish you for all sins, that he might bring you to repen-

tance and amendment of life. God's rods have more encouragement to a wise heart than discouragement to them.

The *Indian Dialogues* end with a discourse with a Native American convert to Puritan Christianity, who is concerned about the spiritual state of his people. This convert relates that his tribal people "now have had but a small measure of respect" for him. He is encouraged by the Puritans to "stay a while" at the praying town of Natick and to "adjoin yourself to the church." Later, accompanied by some Bible teachers and with the support of the governor and magistrates of the Massachusetts Bay Colony, it is suggested that he will be able to return to his people "in the service of Jesus Christ."

As we have seen in earlier chapters, racial prejudice and European expansion brought death and destruction to Native American communities in New England. The resulting King Philip's War (1675–1676) destroyed the "praying towns," although John Eliot tried to protect his converts and opposed the enslavement of Native American captives. As red-white relations continued to deteriorate, Rev. Eliot himself was hated by aggressive and bigoted colonists because he defended the Native Americans. What appeared to be a growing Native American Christian movement was devastated in the process of mass incarceration and inhumane treatment.

Believers and nonbelievers in Native American communities were relocated onto reservations and starved in the winter of 1675–1676. Suspicions about all Native Americans ruled the day. Hatred was rampant. Only four praying towns were rebuilt, and even they were only shadows of the former enclaves. Natick, for example, had only ten Native American church members by the end of the century. In his seventies, Rev. John Eliot attempted to pick up the pieces of his work and to rebuild Native American trust. Although nearly half of his converts remained faithful to the Christian religion (in spite of the fact that they were quite disillusioned with white "Christians"), they were scattered and scarred. Eliot died without a suitable replacement to expand upon his work in eastern Massachusetts. And yet, four decades later, a similar enterprise was attempted in western Massachusetts among the Housatonic Mahican tribes.

Roger Williams

No one is quite sure today about the date of Roger Williams' birth, but he is believed to have been born around 1603. It is known that he was born in London, the son of a shopkeeper, and that he was educated at Cambridge University. A religious nonconformist, Williams sailed into Boston harbor on February 5, 1631. In 1633 he became the minister of the church in Salem. By this time, Rev. Williams was in trouble with the Boston church authorities because he advocated religious freedom for all and asserted that the royal charter did not justify the English colonists taking land that belonged to Native Americans.

Puritan authorities in the Massachusetts Bay Colony determined to send Roger Williams back to England, but he escaped to a wilderness area that would later become Rhode Island. It was Rev. Roger Williams who founded the town of Providence and established a government based on the consent of the settlers. Williams purchased the land from the Native Americans in the area and with their full consent built the town. He became good friends with the Native Americans in this territory and compiled a dictionary of their language. He had a respect for Native American rights and culture that transcended most of his fellow Puritans.

Roger Williams is an example of the few Christian colonial leaders who believed that equitable dealings with Native Americans, including just dealings in the important area of land settlement, were in the best interest of the colonists and the emerging nation. He also believed that fairness and kindness were the Christian models of interaction and communication. Nevertheless, he had to travel to England in 1643 to obtain a royal charter to safeguard his colony against the encroaching New England colonies. Ironically, he had to accept the type of royal charter that in principal he had argued against when he arrived in the New World.

Williams did succeed, however, in getting Governor Winthrop of the Massachusetts Bay Colony to purchase land directly from recognized Native Americans (although the colonial court system had ruled that the royal charter superseded native rights), and set the stage for Christians such as Samuel Sewall (1652–1730) to work for a more enlightened policy toward the local tribes. Samuel Sewall, a prominent Massachusetts judge and landholder as well as an official in the Society for the Propagation of the Gospel in New England, opposed legislation that would harm Native American rights and insisted that Native Americans be protected from colonial encroachment. The presiding judge at the Salem Witchcraft Trials in 1692, Sewall would publicly confess five years later that he was to blame more than other judges for the execution of the twenty "witches," and asked forgiveness of God and man. Judge Samuel Sewall was appointed Chief Justice of the Superior Court of Judicature in the Massachusetts Bay Colony in 1718, a position from which he valiantly tried to protect Native Americans.

The precepts set by Roger Williams were also evident in the actions of the English Quaker, William Penn (1644–1718), a graduate of Oxford University. Penn's three letters to the eastern Iroquois tribes in Pennsylvania in the early 1680s are examples of the most advanced concepts of Native American rights in the Colonial Period and exhibit a deep respect for tribal people. William Penn declared that all trade relations and land transactions with Native Americans were to be conducted in a spirit of love, friendship, and justice. Courts were to be composed of individuals from both peoples, and Native Americans were to be thoroughly protected under the law. Native Americans returned the love and respect that Penn had shown them. A series of amicable treaties were signed between 1682 and 1701. A fifty-year period of peace ensued and Native Americans never attacked Penn's colony, even in the worst of times.

Samson Occom

Samson Occom (1723–1792), a full-blooded Mohegan, was perhaps the greatest Christian Native American evangelist and preacher of the eighteenth century. A product of the religious revivalism of the Great Awakening that swept the colonies in the latter 1730s and early 1740s, Samson Occom decided to enter the ministry and became the special educational project of Eleazar Wheelock (1711–1779), a Congregational revivalist and educator. Rev. Wheelock often tutored colonial students who were preparing for college, and in 1743 he began tutoring young Samson Occom. Impressed by Occom's intelligence, discipline, religious fervor, facility for languages and grasp of ideas, Wheelock envisioned the future Christianization of Native Americans through education and separation from tribal influences. He developed a coeducational boarding school program that would prepare young men for missionary service to their own people—young women also, who would assist the men "in the Business of their mission."

The program was ill-suited for Native American lifestyle, and any success Samson Occom and other graduates of Moor's Charity School obtained was often in spite of Wheelock's educational practices. Rev. Wheelock had the students up before sunrise, cleaned and dressed for morning prayers and Bible reading. After breakfast, chores, and manual labor training, the students were rigorously drilled in Greek classics and ancient languages. Wheelock was adamant that his students should memorize Virgil, the Roman poet, and should also learn to read Latin, Greek, and Hebrew. He felt that this was the method by which the students would spread "Christian civilization" to their tribes; he maintained that method for twenty-five years. Most students rebelled against his rigid regimen; others despaired, became depressed, and succumbed to illness. A few died. Samson Occom was his shining example of what could be accomplished with a Native American, and was used successfully as a fundraiser among white colonists for Rev. Wheelock's ministry.

Licensed by the Presbyterian church to preach, Samson Occom proved to be an excellent missionary to Native Americans and a fine preacher. Nevertheless, he was made to labor and prove his calling for twelve years before the Presbytery of Long Island (made up of white ministers) finally and officially ordained him as a Presbyterian minister in 1759. By this time he had successfully evangelized throughout the Long Island area and had garnered wide acclaim among his Native American people. Although he preached in several locations each week, he also taught school, pastored several congregations, officiated at weddings and funerals, and provided care for young people as well as hospitality for scores of visitors. He also crafted articles for sale to supplement his meagre income and even learned to bind and restore old books. From 1761–1763 he embarked on missionary journeys to the Oneida tribes in central New York. In 1766 Rev. Wheelock asked him to travel to England for two years to solicit funds to support his Indian school. The British were very impressed with the Native American preacher, Samson Occom, and gave generously. Rev. Occom returned with more than 12,000 pounds.

To Samson Occom's great disappointment, Rev. Eleazar Wheelock had become discouraged with Native American response to his educational program. Rev. Wheelock took the funds that Occom had collected in Britain, moved to New Hampshire, and founded a school basically for whites named after the Earl of Dartmouth, another patron. Rev. Wheelock then became Dartmouth College's first president. Samson Occom was outraged that funds for a Native American school were misused, and he broke relations with Wheelock from that day forward. Rev. Wheelock tried to rationalize his actions by conducting a small nominal indian education program through Dartmouth, but after his death Dartmouth College became an all-white institution. Rev. Samson Occom continued his valiant ministry, in spite of the decimation of the east coast tribes. In 1784 he led a remnant of his parishioners to a new settlement called Brothertown in central New York. It was six miles from New Stockbridge, another settlement of displaced Christian Native Americans.

Stockbridge

In western Massachusetts, representatives of the Boston government conferred with the Housatonic Mahicans on the possibility of building a Christian mission in their valley. Ministers felt that these Native American tribes were distanced from evil European influences and would provide a fertile field for evangelization. Authorized in the summer of 1734, the township of Stockbridge was purchased and established for Christian converts and those Native Americans interested in Christianity. A 1729 Yale graduate who had tutored at Yale until 1735, Rev. John Sergeant, dedicated fourteen years of his life to the Housatonic Mahicans.

An ordained Congregationalist minister, Sergeant convinced the Massachusetts government to provide a meeting-house, school, and schoolmaster for his charges. Teaching the children by day and the adults in the evening, Rev. Sergeant concentrated on converting the Native Americans while instilling "civilized" habits. He translated Bible passages, the Shorter Catechism, and a variety of prayers into the Mahican language, while continuing his efforts to get the tribe to learn English. Upon his untimely death at the age of 39, John Sergeant had baptized 182 Mahicans, accepted 42 into church membership, and had been granted funds to establish a boarding school for Native American boys and girls.

These Christian natives of the Housatonic Valley became recognized as a separate tribe called the Stockbridge nation. Rev. John Sergeant's death did not spell the end to the Stockbridge experiment; but rather it encouraged the Society for Propagating the Gospel among the Indians in New England to build on his labors. None other than the famed theologian of the First Great Awakening, Jonathan Edwards, came to Stockbridge in 1751. More than a decade after revivals had swept his church and surrounding areas, Edwards was dismissed from his famous Northampton congregation over disputes concerning ministerial authority and church discipline. For seven years after his arrival in Stockbridge, Rev. Edwards preached to the Native American Christians through an interpreter. It appears that Jonathan Edwards was more interested in developing additional theological treatises for the white community rather than in learning or working with Native American culture. In 1758 he was called back to the east to take the presidency of the College of New Jersey (Princeton University).

The French and Indian War in the mid-1750s killed a large number of Stockbridge males as these Native American Christians attempted to help the English. Unfortunately, Stockbridge was on one of the main French invasion routes. When John Sergeant, Jr., arrived in 1775 to resume his father's work among the Stockbridge nation, he found a much smaller

Native American community. Other pressures absorbed his time as young Sergeant provided ministerial guidance during the next decade. White greed had surfaced once again. A well-meaning plan was circumvented.

The fatal flaw in what appeared to be another noble Puritan religious experiment among Native Americans was that the Massachusetts legislature had given allotments to four English Christian families. These white families were supposed to be examples of civilized English practices, moral Christian fortitude, and pious Puritan lifestyle that Native American converts could look forward to emulating as they matured in Christ. Alas, these families and their white compatriots would eventually displace the Native Americans in the Housatonic Valley in a far from "Christian" manner.

Accompanied by Rev. John Sergeant, Jr., the Stockbridge nation was forced in 1786 to move to central New York. On lands ceded to the Stockbridge nation by the Oneida tribes in central New York, tribes who had also been evangelized, leaders of the Stockbridge nation built "New Stockbridge." These Native American Christians of the Stockbridge nation were taught far different lessons than the Puritans in the Massachusetts legislature and Massachusetts churches had envisioned. By the end of the Revolutionary War, most of the remnants of the New England tribes had begun a westward migration in response to White pressure and to preserve the integrity of their families.

Some Native Americans fought for the new nation called the United States of America. It appears that the Delaware tribes were even offered the prospect of statehood in a negotiated treaty (an "Indian State" that never materialized). Christian missions among the Delaware tribes had flourished, as missionaries such as Presbyterian David Brainerd (1718–1747) and his brother John Brainerd (d. 1781) labored among them. One of the first treaties between the new nation and Native Americans was signed with the Delawares at Pittsburgh. Nevertheless, Delawares too were moved west. In 1801 the last of the New Jersey Christian Delawares sold their reservation and joined other refugees at New Stockbridge. In 1824 Native American remnants of the New Stockbridge Christian communities would be forced to move to Green Bay, Wisconsin. By 1832 the federal government once again confiscated their land and moved them to Indian Territory in Oklahoma.

During the Revolutionary War in 1778, George Washington sought a Native American contingent of four hundred troops for scouts and light infantry. Mixed throughout his troops, General Washington felt that he could make "excellent use" of these warriors. Native Americans suffered terribly within and without the revolutionary armed forces. During the terrible winter at Valley Forge, Dr. Waldo, a surgeon, wrote that he "was called to relieve a soldier of General Washington's thought to be dying," but that the soldier had "expired" before Waldo arrived. "He was an Indian, an excellent soldier," Dr. Waldo related, thoughtfully adding, "and has fought for the very people who disinherited his forefathers."

▼ Mistreatment and Martyrdom

Conversion did not prevent forced expulsion to the west. As we have seen, Native American Christians suffered horribly. In addition, the move west did not prevent the destruction and death of converted Native Americans. A new page in the annals of Christian martyrdom was added by European execution of Native American Christians—a martyrdom that is rarely catalogued by church historians.

For example, in 1782 Christian Delawares were massacred at Gnadenhutten in an area that was to become the State of

Ohio. In an act of Christian charity and peace, these Delaware tribespeople had left their cultivated and planted fields at Gnadenhutten to avoid conflict with white farmers. Along with other villages founded by Moravian missionary David Zeisberger (1721–1808) and his colleagues, Christian Native American men, women, and children moved to Sandusky. Their old fields had to be harvested, however, to feed their families. A portion of the tribe returned to harvest the grain and to collect their possessions. Confronted by U.S Colonel David Williamson and one hundred militiamen from Fort Pitt who happened to be patrolling the area, the Native Americans explained what they were doing and surrendered. Colonel Williamson and his men then tied up the Native American men, women, and children and, to save ammunition, proceeded to club them to death, scalp them, and burn them. Williamson and his white compatriots brutally murdered 29 men, 27 women, and 34 children. Eyewitnesses recorded that the unresisting Christian Native Americans sang hymns and prayed as they were inhumanly slaughtered.

The peaceful and industrious Christian communities of Native Americans founded by Moravian missionaries at Lichtenau, Schonbrunn, and Salem in Ohio (as well as Gnadenhutten) earlier had been forced to move west of the Ohio River by abusive and unrelenting white settlers. Now they and their European missionaries were forced north into Canada. New Gnadenhutten was founded in Ontario. With a deep seated missionary zeal, David Zeisberger returned to the United States to build mission stations and to preach. "There are so many other places where God's Word ought to be preached," Zeisberger would often lament, "so many Indians who have not yet heard that their Maker is their Redeemer." After more than six decades among the Native Americans, however, David Zeisberger watched helplessly as more atrocities devastated his converts and younger missionaries gave up in discouragement. In his eighties, and too old to travel from mission to mission, he watched as his American flock was ravaged and dispersed by a nation on the move.

Nineteenth- and twentieth-century Protestant Christian missions to Native Americans magnified some of the best and most of the worst of the colonial enterprise. There were always some white Christians who fought against stripping tribes of their culture, saw value in the Native American way of life, sought to understand their Native American brothers and sisters, and fought against deceptive and evil actions by other whites. Samuel Austin Worcester and Elihu Butler, whom we viewed in the introduction to this chapter opposing the State of Georgia on behalf of the Cherokee Nation in the 1830s, were two of these faithful Christian friends. Native American communities responded to such sensitivity and were willing to listen to a gospel that was backed up by a visible Christian life.

But more often than not, Christians were immersed in the civil religion of their century, a civil religion that clouded the best that the Christian message has to offer. Many missionaries agreed with the efforts of the federal government to "civilize" and "assimilate" Native Americans into the mainstream of American citizenship and culture. In fact, subsidies from the American government were given to a number of missionary groups when they convinced the politicians that conversion to Christianity and proper religious influences would "Americanize the aborigines." A number of treaties specified that part of the funds allotted to tribes would be used to support missionaries to Native Americans and the tools of civilization that they needed to "civilize the savage," from Presbyterian mission schools to Methodist agricultural training implements for missionary sponsored farms.

In 1819 Congress passed a bill that established a "civilization fund" of 10,000 dollars a year that missionary organizations and evangelists could dip into to link assimilation efforts with conversion efforts. A year earlier, the House Committee on Indian Affairs recommended this bill with smug feelings of cultural superiority and traces of civil religion, a religion of Americanization. The committee declared in part the following:

> Put into the hands of their [Native American] children the primer and the hoe, and they will naturally, in time, take hold of the plow; and as their minds become enlightened and expand, the Bible will be their book, and they will grow up in habits of morality and industry, leave the chase [tribal patterns of hunting, trapping, herding, fishing, etc.] to those of minds less cultured, and become useful members of society.

Initially supported by President James Monroe and his Secretary of War, John C. Calhoun, this "civilization fund" that supported missionaries and religious benevolent societies was in use until 1873. The colonial efforts of linking mission schools with assimilation, religious education with white culture, continued throughout the 1800s and well into the twentieth century.

It should be noted that as the "Century of Evangelicalism" (and the historian-dubbed "Benevolent Empire" that was an important part of it) developed during the 1800s, western missionary enterprises throughout the world often exhibited the same cultural elitism. Indigenous missions that value the culture of the people and cultivate Christian native leaders over churches, and organizations that work within native culture are basically the product of the last few decades (with a number of scattered exceptions). Today, missiologists critique in the same manner many American missionary enterprises and actions that have occurred throughout the world.

Thus, it is an interesting fact that the American Board of Commissioners for Foreign Missions (ABCFM), established in 1810 as an interdenominational agency for efforts overseas, spent half of its funds before 1820 for evangelical work among Native Americans in North America. Presbyterian and Congregational missionaries supported by the ABCFM insisted that their educational efforts were to instill "those habits of sobriety, cleanliness, economy, and industry, so essential to civilized life." Other missionaries bragged that they combined the benefits of civilization and the blessings of Christianity, looking forward to the day when the savage would be converted into the citizen, the Indian hunter would become a mechanic, and the Indian village would become a work shop.

Missionaries did, however, disagree about the use of Native American languages in evangelical work. Some agreed with the famed Puritan leader, Cotton Mather, who in 1710 declared that "the best thing we can do for our Indians is to Anglicize them" and that even Native American language was "ill suited" to "the design of Christianity." Others emphasized Native American languages for missionary work and fought the federal government when it periodically declared use of such languages illegal. Throughout this book we have noted missionary efforts and sacrifices to translate the Bible into a variety of Native American languages. Nevertheless, the English language was more often than not viewed as a tool of acculturalization and assimilation in mission schools, and the attempt was made to *replace* Native American languages with English (not to preserve bilingualism and heritage).

It must be remembered that Richard Henry Pratt's sinister educational assimilation efforts (see chapter four) were supported by well-meaning American Christians, who delighted in how polished and Americanized the "Indian savages" had become. And, throughout the nineteenth century and into the twentieth century, American Christian missionaries were often used by government officials to help facilitate treaties and land deals that were not in the best interest of their Native American converts. Many of these missionaries were flattered that their country needed them, and patriotism and civil religion once again overshadowed their higher calling. Pratt, who thought of himself as a Christian gentleman, used an "end justifies the means" approach with Chief Spotted Tail when attempting to talk the chief into sending Native American children to Pratt's school in 1879.

Spotted Tail had no intention of parting with any of the tribe's children, but Pratt cunningly pointed out that Spotted Tail's tribe had been cheated in treaties because of the lack of knowledge of the English language. The children, argued Pratt, could be trained and returned to help their tribe. As we have seen, the argument worked; but Richard Henry Pratt had no intention of returning those children to their tribes and families. Sadly, in a similar manner Christian missionaries throughout the nineteenth and twentieth centuries have succumbed to the beguiling "the end justifies the means" philosophy.

▼ Twentieth-Century Encounters

Native American Christians have suffered countless losses (along with their unconverted brothers and sisters) through such manipulative practices by often well-meaning Christians. Even as a strong Christian voice for Native American rights and culture emerged in the twentieth century, a protracted struggle waged between Christian advocates of assimilation and Christian advocates against assimilation. As late as 1958, over one-third of the White Protestant workers among Native Americans advocated complete assimilation.

Among Roman Catholic missionaries, the number of strong advocates for assimilation approached 45 percent. Only about 10 percent of both Roman Catholic and Protestant White workers held Native American culture in high esteem and wanted it preserved.

In spite of the fact that by the 1990s a large number of Protestant denominations insisted that Native American religions could be reconciled with Christianity, and stated that Native American Christians should be encouraged to rediscover the positive values of their culture, they have been slow to transfer power over missions and missionary enterprises to Native American Christian leaders. In the last two decades Native Americans have protested the paternalism so evident in Protestant missionary enterprises, claiming that they have been treated as inferiors and given subordinate places in administrative decisions and control.

In contrast, the Native American Church with its use of the small, spineless cactus *peyote* as a medical cure and sacramental element claims as much as 10 percent of the tribal population in its "Peyote Way," a blend of ancient religion and Christian theology. Recently, a number of denominations, as well as the National Association of Evangelicals, have supported the Native American Church in its fight for religious freedom and its right to use *peyote* as part of its sacred sunset to sunrise ritual. Other ancient tribal religious rites are currently being practiced from urban areas to reservations by Native Americans who are seeking to bond with their ancient roots. Such efforts have even pierced the U.S. prison system. Since the mid-1970s Native American inmates of state prisons in nineteen western states have won the right to conduct tribal religious ceremonies. As late as March 1989, a federal district judge overturned the Utah state prison system's prohibition of tribal religious ceremonies, and Native American inmates from New Mexico to Oklahoma now participate in the sweat lodge ceremony of purification and meditation.

Mormons colonized millions of acres of Native American land in the nineteenth century, and their missionaries established a number of Indian missions. The Mormons (The Church of Jesus Christ of Latter-Day Saints) believed in assimilation of the Native Americans so strongly, however, that they were willing to forgo converts until Native Americans "learned" modern civilization. Although the *Book of Mormon* taught that Native Americans were important geneologically as descendants of the ten lost tribes of Israel, Mormon missionaries were trained in a program of total assimilation and integration for their Native American converts. By the mid-1970s nearly 300 Mormon missionaries were working with 150 Native American mission branches in the United States and Canada. By 1990 over 100 Native Americans had been added to the Mormon missionary staff, more than double the number from the 1970s.

Today, the Mormon university, Brigham Young, has a larger number of Native Americans enrolled in its programs than any other American university, although it has been accused of segregating its Native American Mormons to prevent intermarriage. In fact, Elder George P. Lee, a 46-year-old Navajo and the only Native American to hold a leading position in the hierarchy of The Church of Jesus Christ of Latter-Day Saints, was excommunicated in 1989 for accusing the Mormon leadership of racism and teaching false doctrine. Lee had written that recent Mormon teaching "encourages an attitude of superior race, white supremacy, racist attitude, pride, arrogance, love of power and no sense of obligation to the poor, needy and afflicted." In contrast, exotic inclusivistic religious movements, such as the Bahai movement that originated in nineteenth-century Persia, have made inroads into Native American communities. Calling for all religions to unite in a witness of brotherhood, the universalistic Bahais have shown a deep respect for Native American religion, winning some tribal members.

Christianity has made slow progress among fullblooded Native Americans during the twentieth century. In 1923, Gustavus E. E. Lindquist in his book, *The Red Man in the United States*, reported that a 1921 survey found 26 Protestant denominations engaged in Native American missionary enterprises, supporting 428 pastors and evangelists in 597 churches and mission stations throughout the United States. Nearly all of these religious leaders were White. These churches and mission stations were involved in some manner with 167 reservations, having a total number of 32,164 Native American Christians in their congregations and membership. Nearly three decades later Lindquist's study *Indians in Transition* (1951) noted that in 1950 the Protestant denominations involved in missionary enterprises to Native Americans had escalated to 36, but the Native American Christians in their congregations and membership had increased to only 39,200. Today, it is estimated that 92 percent of the Native Americans on reservations do not attend church.

While a number of mainline denominations are struggling in their ministries among the Native American communities, pentecostal and charismatic movements are growing. Rev. Mike Peters of Ottawa tribal background was encouraged by Assemblies of God pastors to reach out to the four thousand Native Americans in Grand Rapids, Michigan. His Native American Assembly of God storefront congregation is approaching one hundred regular attendees. The Assemblies of God Home Mission Division declared the last decade of the twentieth century the "Native American Decade of Harvest."

Ordained in 1951 by the Oklahoma District of the Assemblies of God, Rev. Simon Peter of Choctaw tribal background preached at revival meetings across the west while pastoring a number of Assemblies congregations in Oklahoma, Arkansas, Texas, and Colorado. In 1978 Rev. Peter became the first Native American president of the American Indian Bible Institute in Phoenix, Arizona. He and other Native American Christians influenced the Intercultural Ministries Department of the Division of Home Ministries of the Assemblies of God to take a more careful look at the plight of Native Americans. Rev. Simon Peter left a family of strong and dedicated Christians. His son, Rev. William Earl Peter, pastors the Latham Assembly of God in Shady Point, Oklahoma.

For the most part, the religious groups that are growing among Native Americans are groups that respect the Native American past and the Native American culture. These groups are among the few in history willing to take the time to learn about the dynamism of the Native American community and the vibrancy of their tradition. They have accepted the challenge to understand what makes Native Americans operate as a people and what constitutes the Native American essence. They understand that for the Native American "religion" is "a way of life."

The religious encounter between those of European stock and those of Native American stock was a one-sided encounter. Although Native Americans had much to offer and much to teach (as will be seen in the next chapter), their dynamic community was ignored, maligned, and massacred. For the Native American, practice was far more important than preachments—an honorable life far more important than theological systems. Unfortunately they saw few positive White traits to emulate and embrace. They believed that "White" was equated with "Christian," that "White culture" was "Christian civilization." Missionaries as well as governmental emissaries too often taught the same equation. Those

Native Americans who did embrace Christ as their savior did so at great cost and often in spite of the actions of "Christians."

In 1890, in the midst of the Ghost Dance religious fervor among the Sioux, the *Chicago Tribune* suggested in an editorial that "if the United States army would kill a thousand or so of the dancing Indians there would be no trouble." Before this suggestion was partially fulfilled the same year in the Wounded Knee Massacre, a Sioux brave named Masse Hadjo sent a letter to the editor of the *Chicago Tribune*, declaring that by the wording of the editorial the newsman was probably a "Christian" and doubtless "disposed to do all in your power to advance the cause of Christ." The Sioux man was incensed that the editor wanted freedom of worship for Christians, but would not let the Native Americans have freedom of religious expression.

"The Indians have never taken kindly to the Christian religion as preached and practiced by the whites," Masse Hadjo declared, later explaining in his letter that "the code of morals as practiced by the white race will not compare with the morals of the Indians." Pointing out the crime and sin so prevalent in White culture, as well as the persecution and death that Whites dispensed on those who did not believe as they believed, the Sioux man ended by suggesting that "if the white man's hell suits you, why, you keep it. I think there will be white rogues enough to fill it."

6

▲▼▲   ▲▼▲

THE DYNAMIC COMMUNITY: PROBLEMS AND PROSPECTS

Psychoanalyst Erik Erikson's work has stimulated much interest in developmental psychology because it deals with the whole life span of a human being. Although his work has been criticized by some, Erikson's contention that human development occurs in eight "psychosocial stages" has been quoted with affection more often than it has been demeaned. When African-American Professor Alvin Poussaint is questioned about the black concept of self, he invariably discusses Erik Erikson. When Professor Elizabeth Douvan talks about the role of women in America, she refers to Erikson's stage of autonomy. And famed Harvard professor and psychiatrist, Dr. Robert Coles, gives credit to Erik Erikson for helping him to chart his work for over three decades, documenting the thoughts and lives of children from all segments of society (from tribal villages to migrant worker camps to ghettos).

Erik Erikson developed his eight stages of human beings from his anthropological work among two Native American tribes: the Sioux and the Yurok. He chose these tribes because of the differing environments from which they came. The

141

142 NATIVE AMERICAN VOICES

Sioux roamed the plains and hunted, while the Yurok lived in mountainous regions and fished. Erikson's goal was to ascertain the impact of training and education in each tribe's child rearing. He also wanted to know how a society could make adjustments after their culture had been subjected to a "forced" way of life. In the process, Erik Erikson came to have great respect for the influence of Native American cultural passages and rites. His theories emphasized the importance of cultural environmental influences in contrast to biological influences. It was a dynamic community that Erik Erikson found in traditional Native American culture.

▼ Traditional Native American Life Stages

One is impressed with traditional Native American parenting when one compares the positive attributes of Erik Erikson's psychosocial stages with the traditional Native American attitudes toward development of the human being. According to Erikson's view, a newborn's first awareness is of physical needs. If the child's caretaker anticipates and consistently fulfills these needs during the first year, the infant will learn TRUST.

In traditional Native American culture, children were seen as a valued aspect of life and as important components of the tribe. Children went everywhere with the mother, often tied to her back. The mother would speak to the infant in a normal fashion, never using "baby talk," but rather treating each child as an individual. The entire tribal community served as an extended family to the child, and some teaching actually was coupled to trust during the first year of life.

According to Erikson, the second stage of development is between two and three years of age. While the muscular and nervous systems are developing rapidly, a child has the opportunity to learn AUTONOMY (independence) in the best sense of the concept. The child's judgment, however, has not developed as rapidly as these other systems, potentially endangering the health and safety of the child. Children are eager to acquire new skills and to explore their surroundings. Too much freedom through permissiveness may overwhelm them, detracting from a developing sense of independence. On the other hand, too much control may cause the child to doubt himself or herself, engendering feelings of worthlessness and shame.

Traditional Native American culture maintained a balance between freedom and control by giving the child minimal jobs that they could handle. Opportunities abounded to learn responsibility, and through rituals and tribal activities the children gained a sense of pride in who they were and what they represented. Native American children were taught the tribal language, enlisted in physical activities, and assessed as to where their talents and skills lay. Native Americans believed that the child's questions were a great vehicle to the growth and development of a well-rounded human being. Each member of the extended tribal family (from young adults to the elderly) spent time teaching the children about the harmony of nature and the harmony of the community.

During the development years of four to five, Erikson felt that children enter into the third stage. Once the sense of autonomy or independence has been sufficiently developed, children want to explore their capabilities. Vigorous play and fantasy come into life at this stage as children envision that they are hunters, fishermen, basket weavers, mothers, fathers, warriors, and so on. A proper parental response to these actions could develop INITIATIVE in each child.

In traditional Native American culture the child's exploration was viewed as a creative effort. The child's self-expression was given latitude within a safe tribal environment. Creations by the child were not to be viewed as "a mess," and help that the child gave was welcomed as a contribution rather than a hindrance or necessary evil. A sense of confidence, and an individualism within the communal context was engendered in each child by the age of five. More freedom of ideas was allowed and ancestral teachings were correlated with the child's individual thoughts.

Between the ages six to 12 Erikson believed that INDUSTRY could be developed with the proper encouragement. During this fourth stage the child has a greater attention span and is gaining in strength. The child is ready to expend even more effort in acquiring skills. In Native American culture (as for Erik Erikson) readiness was the key. Responsibilities began to change as the child grew and was assessed. Training began in earnest as the child was gently directed to find his or her role in the tribal community. Harsh criticism of the child was not permitted. Roles were not limited, but accomplishments were praised and abilities were respected. For example, it was during this time period that the children were allowed to sit on the outer limits of the council fire and to view the practice of dialogue and decision-making.

Erikson believed that when a child reached his or her teen years (at times even earlier), a strong IDENTITY could be developed during a fifth stage. The well-balanced teenager recognized continuity and sameness in their personality even when the situation changed or they encountered a variety of individuals. As we have seen in previous chapters, the traditional Native American attitude was to give the teenager opportunities to use their skills and provide tribal rituals to mark their entrance into maturity. Rites of passage, such as the vision quest for the young male, not only engendered harmony and identity in the present life, but also emphasized the afterlife. The young female also participated in proscribed rituals that celebrated her womanhood and underscored her devotion to purity. In fact, teenagers danced, sang, performed rituals, and entered into a fuller religious experience, fasting and praying with the community. Identity was constantly being shaped and affirmed. In Native American cultures the teenager was "promised" in marriage (or entered into marriage) during this time period.

Erik Erikson's sixth stage is the stage of young adulthood, from approximately ages 19–43. The fusing of identity with another individual would lead to INTIMACY. Traditionally, through marriage and children of their own, the young adults directly contributed to the life and livelihood of the tribal community. Interaction is more pronounced, and because a sense of trust, participation, and continuity has been established in earlier years, the man or woman does not experience a midlife crisis of confusion and isolation. A sense of ever-learning has been established as well, and the young adult continues to develop and participate. By nurturing and raising children of their own, the young adults actively maintained a strong and positive traditional culture.

The seventh stage is one of middle age (44–69). According to Erikson, this stage should be one of ever-broadening concern. One's interests expand to include the next generation, in fact, the whole of humanity. This results in what Erikson called GENERATIVITY. In traditional Native American culture these middle-aged individuals participated in an extended family to care for and teach the young. They cherished the opportunity to pass on the rich heritage and wealth of experience to a future generation of leaders and active tribal participants. Instruction in morals as well as character was to be by example. Deeds were as important as words.

The eighth stage is old age (70 plus). Acceptance of one's life led to a sense of INTEGRITY. In traditional Native American culture, the test and background of one's approach to death was how one had lived one's life. Honor and dignity were an elderly Native American's last gift to family and community.

▼ Constructs and Comparisons

In the traditional setting, Native Americans sought as parents, individuals, and community to develop young men and women who could be a positive contribution to their community. The emphasis was on developing the particular talents and skills of the young person to make them successful within the community structure, while at the same time developing each one's trust, autonomy, initiative, industry, and identity. This was in distinct contrast to European culture, which sought to emphasize the complete success of the individual and the importance of creating an individual domain.

The use of the concept of "active parenting" is popular in modern psychology, counseling, and social work today. This concept of parenting by example, however, was practiced in Native American cultures centuries ago. Native Americans imparted knowledge and lessons through a third person, using the spider, coyote, or wayward one to avoid ridiculing a tribal member or causing the loss of self-esteem. For example, if a tribal member was overwhelmed by an addiction or problem, the Native American counselor would share the story of the spider who carefully wraps a web around the unsuspecting victim. The victim struggles on its own, but the strands envelop all the more, soon sapping the strength from the victim. The lesson: a person in trouble needs help from another member of the community to lend a hand in unraveling the stifling strands. For both child and adult, parents and community members were there to help them achieve success in their personal lives as well as to determine their specific talents in tribal life. In this way, each successive age group helped to "parent" community members—guiding them to be all that they could be. Traditional Native American culture emphasized a number of aspects in this pursuit. Religion was important, but was not to be argued about. One thing Native American leaders noticed right away about European religious practice was the division it brought between individuals and communities, the arguments and even deaths that were leveled in the name of Christianity. In Native American culture, religion should never divide a community, but should bring all into harmony. One universal characteristic in traditional Native American religion was that it was never put in a separate realm of one's life, but rather was pervasively present. The sacred was intertwined with all aspects of daily life. A spiritual belief system allowed one to commune with the Creator, while at the same time pursuing one's life purpose and spiritual standing. Native Americans believed that each person must have a spiritual guide to direct into all wisdom and life, to understand and to live. Everything had a purpose, every emotion had a time. Grieving and mourning, fasting and prayer, giving and laughing, all contributed to the fullness of life.

Education was also important, but it was more informal. Everything could be used as a teaching tool. Daily phenomena were used as tools of instruction to illustrate the lessons of life itself. Each time a lesson was taught, however, it was viewed as just the beginning of knowledge. Learning was never "finished," a lesson was never "completed." This educational process was accomplished through both work and play. Games were constructed for all ages and for both sexes. They could go on for days, enhancing agility, stamina, and perseverance. The need for humor, laughter, and smiles was part of participating in the harmony of God's creation. A healthy body led to a healthy mind, and through oral tradition Native Americans taught what one ate, when one ate, and why one ate. Traditional Native American culture taught that one must never waste creation (including food), but to take only what one needed.

The modern concept of holistic medicine actually permeated this ancient Native American culture. In the tribal value system there was no separation between medicine, religion, and culture. All three were interrelated. Physical, mental, emotional, or social illness was thought to be a disharmonious relationship with nature. Although Native American medicines provided many breakthroughs for western physicians, medical practitioners in the Native American world treated the emotional conditions along with the physical ailments. Time was spent with each patient, and it was realized that true healing was more than a dose of antibiotics. Natural herbs from Mother Earth are more valued than synthetic medicines produced in a laboratory, and it is difficult for any outsider to comprehend the intricate connection of the Native American to the Land.

When discussing the "soothing, strengthening, cleansing, and healing" earth, Chief Luther Standing Bear (1868–1939) of the Oglala Sioux would often describe the love and attachment for the soil that grows with age. "This is why the old Indian still sits upon the earth instead of propping himself up and away from its life-giving forces. For him, to sit or lie upon the ground is to be able to think more deeply and to feel more keenly; he can see more clearly into the mysteries of life and come closer in kinship to other lives about him." Indeed, the nineteenth century Yamparika Comanche poet and peacemaker, Ten Bears (1792–1872), prayed:

Great Spirit—I want no blood upon my land to stain the grass. I want it all clear and pure, and I wish it so, that all who go through among my people may find it peaceful when they come, and leave peacefully when they go.

"I love the land and the buffalo and will not part with it," the Kiowa Chief Satanta (c.1830–1878) exclaimed, "there I feel free and happy."

Generosity flowed from this culture. At honoring events, those being honored often gave to the community. This was quite a contrast to European culture, which expected the one honored to be given awards. Even today one must be careful in admiring something of value that a Native American has or it is immediately offered to the guest. This generous spirit led one directly into the realm of respect. Around the council fire, members of the tribal community listened respectfully as another person imparted a viewpoint. A soft but firm voice was better than a loud speech, and a loving, respectful spirit was to permeate all conversation. Teaching as well as speech-making was from the heart. "Silence is the cornerstone of character." Ohiyesa (Charles Alexander Eastman, 1858–1939), a Santee Sioux physician and author of ten books that described Native American life to general audiences, would often explain this. European society wrongly interpreted the Native American's silence as passivity or weakness. Many Europeans could not understand these positive Native American values and lifestyles (although western philosophers, theologians, and their very own Bible taught such concepts).

As we have seen, traditional Native Americans were not perfect. They were human beings, with struggles and failures along the pathways of life. In wars and attacks some groups exhibited their bravery, skills, and toughness. These warriors garnered honor and respect from their communities. Native American veterans of war were never forgotten and never despised. And yet, as we have seen, respect for all life permeated even the war scene. An enemy was respected, and seldom did the Native American have the inclination to move in for the final kill. Once it was evident that an enemy had been defeated it was unnecessary to humiliate and devastate his entire community. Little could the Native Americans know that those from European backgrounds dealt in terms of extermination and massacre.

In fact, it is nearly impossible for the modern social worker, psychologist, government official, or minister to deal effectively with Native Americans without understanding the contrasts between White culture and traditional Native American values. Native Americans emphasize happiness and sharing, while modern society emphasizes success and ownership. Modern concepts of competition, structure, criticism, self-promotion, materialism, persuasion, and a compulsion for "bigness" are foreign to traditional Native American values. The modern emphasis on youthfulness is in distinct contrast to the Native Americans' respect for their elders. To the Native American, the fewer the rules the better, and laws should be flexible. Intuitive and mystical, the traditional Native American seems sadly out of place in our space-age, scientifically-oriented society. And yet many of the values expressed in this traditional culture are values that are an intrinsic part of the Judeo-Christian religious system.

For example, consider Proverbs 20:7, "The just man walks in his integrity. Happy are his children after him"; or Psalm 127:3, "Lo, children are a heritage of the Lord; and the fruit of the womb is a reward." Compare Native American tradition to Romans 15:1–2.

> We then that are strong ought to bear the infirmities of the weak, and not to please ourselves. Let every one of us please his neighbor for his good to building up.

Likewise, one might compare that immortal chapter on love in 1 Corinthians 13, including the words, "Love suffereth long, and is kind; love envieth not; love vaunteth not itself, is not puffed up, does not behave itself unseemly, seeks not her own, is not easily provoked, thinks no evil; rejoices not in iniquity, but rejoices in the truth." And one might well compare Jesus's Sermon on the Mount in Matthew chapters five to seven with traditional Native American wisdom and culture. Clearly, it can be established that the pure Judeo-Christian ethic is much closer to the traditional Native American value system than it is to modern social norms and practice. While Native American Christians do not advocate going back totally to a traditional tribal lifestyle, they do believe that Native Americans should return to their roots, retrieving the best concepts of a value system that builds up the individual within the community and enhances environmental concern.

▼ The Toll of Disruption

In spite of these positive values, our study of the history of pain has shown the devastation that was thrust upon Native American communities across the United States. The European incursion has taken an awesome toll. In many cases the parental structure has been disrupted and the extended family has been ravaged. The worst scenario of Erik Erikson's psychosocial stages developed. In infants, trust gave way to MISTRUST, because of inadequate, inconsistent, or negative care; and DOUBT developed instead of autonomy in children. GUILT replaced initiative, and INFERIORITY was engendered in the place of industry. Because of unstable conditions regarding occupations, lifestyle, and the future, ROLE CONFUSION developed in teenagers and young adults instead of a strong identity. Continuity was not established; the community suffered as each individual suffered; and despair and despondency increased.

Today over one-fourth of all Native American children are separated from their families and placed in institutions, foster homes, or adoptive homes. Native American life expectancy is only around 50 years of age. One out of three Native Americans will be jailed during their lifetime, and one out of two Native American families will have a relative die in jail. Suicide among Native Americans at times has approached seven times the national average, and over three-fourths of Native American suicide cases are alcohol related. In fact, almost all crimes for which Native Americans are imprisoned are committed while the individual is under the influence of alcohol. Also, Native Americans die from alcohol-related diseases at four times the national rate. Fetal Alcohol Syndrome is over thirty times higher in Native Americans than in Whites. Maternal drinking during pregnancy causes mental retardation and birth defects. The average Native American is seven years younger than the national average age, and Native American youth have the highest high school dropout rate of any minority group. Low self-esteem and confused cultural identity make Native American teenagers susceptible to addiction, hopelessness, and juvenile gangs. Large numbers of these young people feel powerless to change their deteriorating situation. Fatalism sets in.

Nearly a century ago, a Native American woman wrote about how poverty and prejudice had destroyed her people. It is a sad fact that her words are as relevant today as they were at the beginning of the twentieth century.

> I am not bitter. I have passed that stage. I only want to say: this is what it was like; this is what it is still like. I know that poverty is not ours alone. Your people have it too, but in those earlier days you at least had dreams, you had a tomorrow. My parents and I never shared any aspirations for a future.

As we approach the twenty-first century, the poverty rate for Native American families is more than twice the rate of the general population, and a large majority of Native Americans have had to leave the reservation in order to find jobs that pay enough to support their families. Over 300,000 Native Americans live in metropolitan areas. Reservations are known for extreme poverty and depravation. Less than 30 percent of the Native Americans ages 16–64 on reservations earn more than 7,000 dollars a year. An equal number (over 160,000) are looking for a job. The main streets of most small reservation communities have seen once thriving businesses closed, adding another psychological as well as economic and social toll.

Just as drug dealers prey upon the children and teenagers of the United States in a lucrative narcotics trade today, previous generations of white frontiersmen, settlers, and government officials used alcohol to addict Native Americans. Initially, Native Americans did not like the taste of alcohol, but grew to use the intoxicants through the persistent offerings by explorers who wanted to show their friendship in making tribal members "feel good," and traders who were bent on arranging lucrative markets. Soon liquor became a valuable consumer product in the European trade with Native American tribes. While European diseases killed millions of Native Americans, alcohol poisoned and disabled tens of thousands of the survivors. The problems persist to this day, because alcohol is the cheapest intoxicant available.

And yet recent studies have shown that popular conceptions of the "drunken Indian" and the "Indian's inherited weakness to alcohol" are only additional myths. The fact is that daily drinking or chronic alcohol addiction is relatively unusual among those on reservations. The percentage is quite low of those tribal members who need alcohol every day. The majority of alcohol problems occur from intermittent bouts of hard drinking, sometimes for days, predominantly by young men. This is a problem for western white "cowboy towns" as well, actually stemming from the binge-drinking patterns of the hard-drinking frontiersmen, prospectors, and soldiers of the Wild West. For the Native American, it is a learned behavior.

There is no scientific evidence to suggest that Native Americans metabolize alcohol any more slowly than Whites. The liver is the main organ responsible for this process, and it is the same in both these groups. In addition, drinking habits vary greatly from tribe to tribe. The stereotypes do not fit, and yet even Native Americans seem to believe the caricatures concerning alcohol. Western Whites, of course, often point to Native American hard-drinking, while turning a blind eye toward the hard-drinking that goes on among their White friends and neighbors. Many of those running tribal alcohol addiction programs and ministering to Native Americans have bought into the myth of genetic weakness to alcohol, hindering effective alcohol treatment.

Indeed, abuse is abuse. Alcohol abuse during "recreational" or "party" drinking bouts is taking a severe toll on Native American communities. It goes hand in hand with the sense of hopelessness and the lack of opportunity for those U.S. citizens on the bottom rungs of the social and economic ladder. Ironically, economic depression on the reservations leads to an acceptance of such recreational "escape." While men and women who are physically and psychologically addicted to alcohol are treated as outcasts on the reservation, the binge drinkers are often accepted and even encouraged by some community members. Since life is so difficult, they rationalize, let the young men have a little fun. For the young men and women who feel alienated, angry, and frustrated, they seek to alter their feelings through a drinking binge.

To make matters worse, beer companies traditionally have targeted reservations with huge advertising campaigns. As one of the few big businesses near tribal homelands, local beer distributors have been involved in the funding or partial funding of Native American celebrations, conferences, and annual events. They require in return huge advertising banners, prominent displays, and adequate facilities to distribute mementos with their company trademarks. In tribal parades, a beer company float may be viewed in the same procession as a float against alcohol abuse. Popular beer mascots have catered to assembled reservation young people, doing tricks and shaking hands with gleeful children. One mascot has been known to toss out to Native American children thousands of miniature rolls of candy packaged as tiny beer cans. That this can occur in the midst of alcohol abuse and abuse prevention programs has not been lost on disturbed tribal members and health officials.

Teenage alcohol consumption is a serious concern among Native Americans, just as it is a major concern among parents of U.S. teenagers in general. On some reservations, however, upwards of 40 percent of the teens report that they abuse alcohol. The problems follow them into early adulthood. Some of the saddest examples have been given by Professor Russell Craig. An expert in the field of social deviance and an experienced veteran in the criminal justice and social welfare system, Professor Craig worked for nearly a decade as a parole officer on South Dakota reservations and had a high regard for Native Americans. In an interview, he confirmed the toll that alcohol abuse can take.

Dr. Craig worked with many of the young men who were in the deepest trouble on the reservation, and he had seen the worst that reservation despair and the breakdown of traditional Native American values could produce. He found that under the influence of alcohol there was a total disregard for human life, including one's own life. Russ Craig explained:

> That is one of the things I found that shocked me so much, I guess, is that as I dealt with the people who got in fights and chopped the other fellow in the head with a shovel, nearly

killing him, and now he's brain damaged for the rest of his life, and the people who abused or killed their children or scalded them to death, or participated in brutal rapes, I found a terrible crudity, and a lot of violence, and a lot of disregard for human life on the reservation. For these persons, social organization was so lacking and family structure so broken down that there were really no rules.

"And it doesn't happen when they are sober," Dr. Craig affirmed from his own experience, "it very frequently occurred when they were drunk."

"And they would do the same things to themselves," Professor Craig quickly added. When bored and drinking, these same young men would play games with cigarettes, seeing how much pain they could endure on their arms as the lighted cigarette burned a hole deep into their flesh. Unlike other Whites who were afraid to pick up a Native American hitch-hiker, Russ Craig almost always gave them a ride because he "felt an obligation to them," and was amazed at all the walking they did. "I never feared an American Indian alone," Dr. Craig related, "only in groups and only if alcohol was involved. And then I didn't necessarily fear them, but I knew I was going to have my hands full."

The Native American's fear of the Public Health Service (which in 1955 took the place of the Bureau of Indian Affairs with regard to governmental medical care) and disregard for their own physical health was often characteristic of the young men Russell Craig met on the road. He told of a Native American hitchhiker he had picked up in the 1970s who was unusually talkative. The man in his midtwenties had two middle fingers that were tied together with several rubberbands. Out of curiosity, Russ Craig asked him, "What did you do to your fingers?"

The young man replied: "Oh, I bent the one backwards playing basketball. I love to play basketball." When the young man took off the rubberbands to show him, the finger flopped completely backwards. He had wrapped it to the other finger for support.

"Why don't you get that fixed?" Russ asked.

"Oh, I don't know. I figure by the time I get it fixed a couple of the others would be broke. I don't really want to go to that PH [Public Health Service] hospital, you know, those butchers might cut it off." The young man was, in fact, hitchhiking to a state hospital in a nearby town to visit his girlfriend.

"Not an unusual experience at all," Dr. Craig confirmed, adding that Native Americans had "good reason" to fear the Public Health Service. Sadly, the young man's girlfriend was in the hospital dying of cirrhosis of the liver from alcohol abuse. She was only 23 or 24 years of age.

One is reminded of an old tribal saying about Native American nations: "A Nation is not conquered until the hearts of its women are on the ground. Then it is done, no matter how brave its warriors nor how strong its weapons." Russ Craig found, however, as we have in our study, that many Native American women have not been conquered and are fighting for their families, their communities, and their traditions. In his dealings with tribal parolees, Dr. Craig found that grandmothers particularly were often bastions of strength and tradition, individuals with whom one could work "if you were honest with them."

"Many winters I have breasted the storm," the noted Seneca warrior and orator, Red Jacket (1756–1830), spoke solemnly of his struggle against the European incursion in the 1700s and his opposition to Anglo-Saxon culture being forced on his people, "but I am an aged tree, and can stand no longer." With his death at hand he explained his plight through this illustration from nature:

> My leaves are fallen, my branches are withered, and I am shaken by every breeze. Soon my aged trunk will be prostrated, and the foot of the exulting foe of the Indian may be placed upon it with safety; for I leave none who will be able to avenge such an injury. Think not that I mourn for myself.

"I go to join the spirits of my fathers, where age cannot come," Red Jacket explained, and then turning to the plight of his people he stated, "but my heart fails when I think of my people, who are soon to be scattered and forgotten."

Little could this Native American leader—who met with President George Washington in 1792 to discuss mutual relations, received a personal presidential medal from Washington, addressed the U.S. Senate, and dealt with a plethora of British and U.S. officials throughout his lifetime—little could he imagine the toll that would be taken . . . or did Red Jacket before his death in 1830 envisage it all too well?

▼ Perceptions and Prospects

The Native American comedian Charlie Hill from the Oneida tribe often questions his White audiences: "How do you think it feels to always be told you were discovered by someone who was lost?" Native Americans have had to deal with a media blitz that has defamed and deformed their heritage. In addition to the historic treatment of Columbus in books and in classrooms, television has had a debilitating affect on the Native American child. Studies in the latter 1950s (the decade in which television spread throughout the United States) showed that Native American children had watched so many deceptive "cowboys and indians" shows on

television that many wished they could be the White cowboy.

Today, a crucial core of Native Americans are attempting
to discard the false information that has been thrust on them
in recent centuries, and they are fighting to regain their communities and their heritage in spite of overwhelming obstacles and the toll that has been taken. It is a formidable task.
Dr. Edwin ("Strong-Legs") Richardson, the first Native American psychologist in the United States, often suggests to his
audiences as well as to government officials and fellow acad-
emicians that the problem is one of values. He states that

> Part of the dilemma in understanding the Indian is that the
> Anglos (Whites) have never thought out their own value sys-
> tem. One exists for Anglos, but because they do things so
> compulsively they do not recognize the noxious qualities of
> their values to themselves or others. Oftentimes the Anglos'
> values are in direct opposition to those of the Indians. The
> majority society has a stereotype of Indians and Eskimos that
> does not reach beneath the surface. The Anglos do not lis-
> ten, and they have been too busy pushing what they consider
> important to be able to listen.

Dr. Richardson teaches his students that successful counselors
among Native Americans must see the positive nature of
traditional tribal values, admit ignorance of Native American
culture (but continue to learn about it), and carefully cultivate
the capacity to listen and observe (rather than "informing"
and "exhorting" in condescending and patronizing fashion).
Adaptability and sincerity are crucial in cultivating Native
American trust and friendship.

Like Dr. Richardson and other experts, Dr. Russell Craig
believes that White "expectations" concerning Native Americans must be adjusted and one must respect the dignity of
the Native American people. Many problems occur when

Native Americans are expected to act like Whites. When governmental officials or officers of the law walk onto a reservation, they must respect the fact that they are strangers in a foreign land. One quietly asserts any perceived authority and must recognize what each individual, family, and community has been through. Honesty is imperative; phoniness is never acceptable.

Church officials must understand that on average it takes five years to be accepted in the Native American community. Changing contacts every two to three years is not effective, and expecting the Native American community to do things as the White community does them is unrealistic. In addition, great strides need to be taken in educating and promoting a caring and qualified Native American leadership of tribal religious enterprises. Religious workers must have the support of their particular denominations in relieving the suffering conditions on the reservations and building up the family structure. This takes dedicated time. This takes sacrificial funds.

The bottom line is to let the Native American community handle its own affairs with adequate funding and no ulterior motives. And, above all, allow Native Americans to fail. Give the reservation leadership the opportunity to make fledgling starts, to have failures as well as successes, to build their society into a self-governing stronghold. Non-Native Americans must understand that even the United States of America as a fledgling immature society had many failures, as well as rampant corruption. Elected U.S. officials failed both in morals and abilities; some U.S. citizens lacked motivation and dedication. Native American society should have the latitude to rebuild and restrengthen in the same manner—to experiment, to implement, and to make some mistakes along the way.

It is exciting today that Native Americans are attempting to start their own industries. The Administration for Native Americans (ANA) based in Washington, D.C., is one of the organizations dedicated to helping Native Americans develop and administrate their own businesses. Tribal colleges are showing promising potential to generate new businesses and jobs, even in areas of science and technology. Some of the new business ventures are directly related to strengthening Native American cultural traditions, and the *powwow* is gaining a central role as a yearly gathering of the Native American nations. In a number of tribes, cultural events based upon traditional ceremonies dot the yearly calendar, creating an annual cycle of traditional values and cultural bonding. High school and college graduation ceremonies are becoming "honoring events" with days of traditional celebrations and group encouragement.

The Cherokee Nation was one of the first tribes to turn down money offered by the beer companies to support cultural events, and a number of Native American communities have since followed suit. The Native American nations are beginning to wage war against the manipulative advertising that has plagued their communities and culture. This war is difficult, because federal funds have been continually cut back in every program, including health services. One of the problems with the Indian Health Service agency of the Public Health Service program of the U.S. Department of Health and Human Services is that its staff is overworked and underfinanced, often making considerate and effective treatment nearly impossible. Many times the work of the agency has to be contracted out to private practices and institutions.

It must be remembered that no Native American is automatically "paid" for being "Indian." Rather, the federal government is obligated by law and decency to compensate a tribe or individual for losses due to treaty violations, for encroachments, or for illegal actions. Nevertheless, legal obligations are sometimes circumvented, stalled, or reinterpreted by a powerful governmental bureaucracy. We are con-

cerned that the more some things supposedly change in this
history, the more the issues appear to remain the same. The
reservations are rich in natural resources, however, and will
be a definite bargaining chip for an ever-emerging dynamic
community. How traditional environmental values will
impact on tribal economic decisions will be a constant struggle for Native Americans in the twenty-first century.

"Knowledge is inherent in all things," Chief Luther Standing Bear believed, "the world is a library." In the past two
decades Native American teachers and administrators have
increased in the nation's public school systems, and the number of public schools controlled by Native Americans has
increased as well. In spite of the failure of existing public or
federal educational systems to effectively meet the cultural,
economic, and social needs of Native American children,
there is every indication that more parents are becoming
involved in the planning, development, and implementation
of educational programs that affect their children. In addition, tribal governments are becoming more active in providing a traditional as well as a modern education, in an effort
to be sensitive to the Native American child's need for roots
while teaching the child to live in two different cultures.
Whenever comprehensive programs and educational curric-
ula have been developed to meet the linguistic, cultural, academic, social, and health needs, Native American children
inevitably develop a more positive self-concept.

The number of Native Americans attending college and
pursuing graduate degrees has been increasing. More Native
Americans are becoming college professors, doctors, lawyers,
psychologists, teachers, engineers, and nurses, as well as
majoring in business, management, computer science, and
public affairs. A number of Native American medical doctors have returned to the reservation area to help their people. There have been numerical gains in associate degrees,

bachelor degrees, master degrees, and doctoral degrees. While these individuals should serve as role models for the Native American community, there is much to be done in the areas of academic preparation, finance, encouragement, and continuing studies. The number of Native Americans attending college is still half of the percentage of other groups. Too often tribal communities allow elementary schools, middle schools, and high schools to perform at minimal standards. Too often Native American professionals are not given the encouragement they need, and technical and service workers do not have the opportunities they need.

Shortly before his death, Sitting Bull talked with school children on the reservation they were forced to endure. The great holy man related the following:

> When I was your age, things were entirely different. I had no teachers but my parents and relatives. They are dead and gone now, and I am left alone. It will be the same with you. Your parents are aging and will die some day, leaving you alone. So it is for you to make something of yourselves, and this can only be done while you are young.

It is important in our estimation that tribal communities take Sitting Bull's words to heart and commit themselves to leading young people into thinking about what they are going to do with their lives *now* (not later). With the disruption of the community and culture, there is no time for the attitude toward teenagers that they should go out, "have fun," and binge. Certainly life is difficult, but advocating that a teenager can think about the deep things in life when he or she is "older" is relegating those young people to a state of unpreparedness and corruption.

Numbering around two million members (with nearly four times that number declaring some Native American "ancestry"), the Native American community in the United States today is a dynamic community that has survived an awesome onslaught. Time and time again we have been reminded of the great potential bubbling below and gushing to the surface in over 500 tribal entities in the United States. Native Americans must take their future into their own hands, but non-Native Americans should be educated to understand their history, their plight, and their current situation. Myths and misinterpretations must be dispelled, for in the end, only a change of opinion and a clear insight by the majority of this land will end the debilitating prejudice that senselessly contributes to the Native Americans' modern history of pain. We have attempted to help you, the reader, on this journey of insight . . . this journey of change.

Continue to contaminate your own bed, and you will one night suffocate in your own waste.—Chief Seattle

Can we talk of integration until there is integration of hearts and minds? Unless you have this, you have only a physical presence, and the walls between us are as high as the mountain range.—Chief Dan George

My friends, how desperately do we need to be loved and to love. . . . Love is something you and I must have. We must have it because our spirit feeds upon it. We must have it because without it we become weak and faint. Without love our self-esteem weakens. Without it our courage fails. Without love we can no longer look out confidently at the world. . . . With love we are creative. With love we march tirelessly. With love, and with love alone, we are able to sacrifice for others.—Chief Dan George

BIBLIOGRAPHY

Anson, Bert. *The Miami Indians.* Norman, Okla.: The University of Oklahoma Press, 1970.

Axtell, James. *Beyond 1492: Encounters in Colonial North America.* New York: Oxford University Press, 1992.

———. *The Invasion Within: The Contest of Cultures in Colonial North America.* New York: Oxford University Press, 1986.

Bataille, Gretchen M., and Kathleen Mullen Sands. *American Indian Women: Telling Their Lives.* Lincoln, Nebr.: University of Nebraska Press, 1984.

Berkhofer, Robert F., Jr. *Salvation and the Savage: An Analysis of Protestant Missions and American Indian Response, 1787–1862.* Lexington, Ky.: University of Kentucky Press, 1965.

———. *Chronicles of American Indian Protest.* New York: The Council on Interracial Books for Children, 1979.

Bowden, Henry W. *American Indians and Christian Missions.* Chicago: The University of Chicago Press, 1981.

Bowden, Henry W., and James P. Ronda. *John Eliot's Indian Dialogues: A Study in Cultural Interaction.* Westport, Conn.: Greenwood Press, 1980.

Brown, Dee. *Bury My Heart at Wounded Knee: An Indian History of the American West.* New York: Bantam Books, 1971.

Brown, Joseph E., ed. *The Sacred Pipe.* Norman, Okla.: The University of Oklahoma Press, 1953.

Bryde, John F. *Modern Indian Psychology.* Vermillion, S. Dak.: University of South Dakota, 1971.

Calloway, Colin G., ed. *Dawnland Encounters: Indians and Europeans in Northern New England*. Hanover, N.J.: University Press of New England, 1991.

Carlson, Leonard A. *Indians, Bureaucrats, and Land: The Dawes Act and the Decline of Indian Farming*. Westport, Conn.: Greenwood Press, 1981.

Colson, Elizabeth. *The Makah Indians: A Study of an Indian Tribe in Modern American Society*. Westport, Conn.: Greenwood Press Publishers, 1974.

Cornell, Stephen. *The Return of the Native: American Indian Political Resurgence*. New York: Oxford University Press, 1988.

Cotterill, R. S. *The Southern Indians: The Story of the Civilized Tribes Before Removal*. Norman, Okla.: University of Oklahoma Press, 1954.

Culin, Stewart. *Games of the North American Indians*. New York: Dover Publications, 1975.

Debo, Angie. *A History of the Indians in the United States*. Norman, Okla.: The University of Oklahoma Press, 1984.

Deloria, Ella C. *Speaking of Indians*. Vermillion, S. Dak.: University of South Dakota, 1944.

Deloria, Vine, Jr. *Behind the Trail of Broken Treaties*. New York: Dell Publishing Company, 1974.

———. *Custer Died For Your Sins*. New York: Avon Books, 1969.

———. *God Is Red*. New York: Dell Publishing Company, 1973.

———. *We Talk, You Listen*. New York: Dell Publishing, 1970.

Deloria, Vine, Jr., ed. *American Indian Policy in the Twentieth Century*. Norman, Okla.: The University of Oklahoma Press, 1985.

Deloria, Vine, Jr., and Clifford M. Lytle. *The Nations Within: The Past and Future of American Indian Sovereignty*. New York: Pantheon Books, 1984.

Dennis, Henry C., ed. *The American Indian, 1492–1976: A Chronology & Fact Book*. Dobbs Ferry, N.Y.: Oceana Publications, Inc., 1977.

DeVoto, Bernard, ed. *The Journals of Lewis and Clark*. Boston: Houghton Mifflin Company, 1953.

Dudley, Joseph Iron Eye. *Choteau Creek: A Sioux Reminiscence.* Lincoln, Nebr.: University of Nebraska Press, 1992.

Eastman, Charles Alexander (Ohiyesa). *The Soul of the Indian.* Boston: Houghton Mifflin Company, 1911.

Edmonds, R. David. *The Potawatomis: Keepers of the Fire.* Norman, Okla.: The University of Oklahoma Press, 1978.

Eggan, Fred. *Social Organization of the Western Pueblos.* Chicago: The University of Chicago Press, 1950.

Erdoes, Richard, and Alfonso Ortiz, eds. *American Indian Myths and Legends.* New York: Pantheon Books, 1984.

Faulk, Odie B. *The Geronimo Campaign.* New York: Oxford University Press, 1993.

Finger, John R. *Cherokee Americans: The Eastern Band of Cherokees in the Twentieth Century.* Lincoln: University of Nebraska Press, 1991.

Foster, Morris W. *Being Comanche: The Social History of an American Indian Community.* Tucson: University of Arizona Press, 1991.

Fritz, Henry E. *The Movement for Indian Assimilation, 1860–1890.* Philadelphia: University of Pennsylvania Press, 1963.

Gibson, Arrell M. *The Chickasaws.* Norman, Okla.: University of Oklahoma Press, 1971.

Goodchild, Peter. *Survival Skills of the North American Indians.* Chicago: Chicago Review Press, 1984.

Goodwin, Grenville. *The Social Organization of the Western Apache.* Tucson, Ariz.: The University of Arizona Press, 1969.

Grant, Bruce. *Concise Encyclopedia of the American Indian.* New York: Bonanza Books, 1958.

Graymont, Barbara. *The Iroquois in the American Revolution.* Syracuse, N.Y.: Syracuse University Press, 1972.

Green, Jesse, ed. *Zuni: Selected Writings of Frank Hamilton Cushing.* Lincoln, Nebr.: University of Nebraska Press, 1979.

Hagan, William T. *The Sac and Fox Indians.* Norman, Okla.: The University of Oklahoma Press, 1958.

Hammerschlag, Carl A. *The Dancing Healers: A Doctor's Journey of Healing with Native Americans.* San Francisco: Harper, 1988.

————. *The Thief of Spirit: A Journey To Spiritual Healing with Native Americans.* New York: Simon & Schuster, 1993.

Harmsen, Bill. *Patterns and Sources of Navajo Weaving.* Denver: Harmsen Publishing Company, 1985.

Harner, Michael. *The Way of the Shaman.* 3rd Ed. San Francisco: Harper, 1990.

Hauptman, Laurence M. *The Iroquois in the Civil War: From Battlefield to Reservation.* Syracuse, N.Y.: Syracuse University Press, 1992.

Hauptman, Laurence M., and James D. Wherry, eds. *The Pequots in Southern New England: The Fall and Rise of an American Indian Nation.* Norman, Okla.: The University of Oklahoma Press, 1990.

Hausman, Gerald. *Turtle Island Alphabet: A Lexicon of Native American Symbols and Culture.* New York: St. Martin's Press, 1992.

Herring, Joseph B. *The Enduring Indians of Kansas: A Century and a Half of Acculturation.* Lawrence: University Press of Kansas, 1990.

Hirschfelder, Arlene, and Beverly R. Singer. *Rising Voices: Writings of Young Native Americans.* New York: Ivy Books, 1992.

Hudson, Charles. *The Southeastern Indians.* Knoxville, Tenn.: The University of Tennessee Press, 1976.

Hyde, George E. *Indians of the High Plains: From the Prehistoric Period to the Coming of Europeans.* Norman, Okla.: University of Oklahoma Press, 1959.

————. *Indians of the Woodlands: From Prehistoric Times to 1725.* Norman, Okla.: University of Oklahoma Press, 1962.

————. *The Pawnee Indians.* Norman, Okla.: University of Oklahoma Press, 1974.

Indian Nations At Risk: An Educational Strategy for Action. Washington, D.C.: U.S. Department of Education, 1991.

Jaffe, A. J. *The First Immigrants from Asia: A Population History of the North American Indians.* New York: Plenum Press, 1992.

Johnston, Charles M., ed. *The Valley of the Six Nations: A Collection of Documents on the Indian Lands of the Grand River.* Toronto: The University of Toronto Press, 1964.

Josephy, Alvin M., Jr. *Red Power: The American Indians' Fight for Freedom.* New York: American Heritage Press, 1971.

———. *The Indian Heritage of America.* New York: American Heritage Press, 1991.

———. *The Nez Perce Indians and the Opening of the Northwest.* New Haven: Yale University Press, 1965.

Kehoe, Alice B. *North American Indians: A Comprehensive Account.* Englewood Cliffs, N.J.: Prentice Hall, 1981.

Kelly, Lawrence. *The Navajo Indians and Federal Indian Policy, 1900–1935.* Tucson, Ariz.: The University of Arizona Press, 1968.

Kupferer, Harriet J. *Ancient Drums, Other Moccasins: Native North American Cultural Adaptation.* Englewood Cliffs, N.J.: Prentice Hall, 1988.

Lame Deer, John (Fire), and Richard Erdoes. *Lame Deer: Seeker of Visions.* New York: Pocket Books, 1972.

Landes, Ruth. *The Mystic Lake Sioux: Sociology of the Mdewakantonwan Santee.* Madison, Wis.: The University of Wisconsin Press, 1968.

Lazarus, Edward. *Black Hills/White Justice: The Sioux Nation Versus the United States, 1775 to the Present.* New York: HarperCollins Publishers, 1991.

Llewellyn, K. N., and E. Adamson Hoebel. *The Cheyenne Way: Conflict and Case Law in Primitive Jurisprudence.* Norman, Okla.: The University of Oklahoma Press, 1941.

Lydekker, John Wolfe. *The Faithful Mohawks.* New York: Ira J. Friedman, Inc., 1938.

McGaa, Ed. *Mother Earth Spirituality.* San Francisco: Harper, 1990.

McNickle, D. *Native American Tribalism: Indian Survivals and Renewals.* New York: Oxford University Press, 1973.

McReynolds, Edwin C. *The Seminoles.* Norman, Okla.: The University of Oklahoma Press, 1957.

Malone, Henry Thompson. *Cherokees of the Old South: A People in Transition.* Athens, Ga.: The University of Georgia Press, 1956.

Marriott, Alice, and Carol K. Rachlin. *Peyote.* New York: New American Library, 1971.

Martin, Calvin, ed. *The American Indian and the Problem of History.* New York: Oxford University Press, 1987.

Mathews, John Joseph. *The Osages: Children of the Middle Waters.* Norman, Okla.: The University of Oklahoma Press, 1961.

Maxwell, James, ed. *America's Fascinating Indian Heritage.* Pleasantville, N.Y.: Reader's Digest, 1978.

Meyer, Roy W. *History of the Santee Sioux: United States Indian Policy on Trial.* Lincoln, Nebr.: University of Nebraska Press, 1967.

Mooney, James. *The Ghost-Dance Religion and the Sioux Outbreak of 1890.* Chicago: The University of Chicago Press, 1965.

Morgan, William N. *Prehistoric Architecture in the Eastern United States.* Cambridge, Mass.: The MIT Press, 1980.

Nabokov, Peter, ed. *Native American Testimony: A Chronicle of Indian and White Relations from Prophecy to Present, 1492–1992.* New York: Penguin Books, 1992.

Nabokov, Peter, and Robert Easton. *Native American Architecture.* New York: Oxford University Press, 1988.

Nash, Gary B. *Red, White, and Black: The Peoples of Early North America.* Englewood Cliffs, N.J.: Prentice Hall, 1992.

Neihardt, John G. *Black Elk Speaks: Being the Life Story of a Holy Man of the Oglala Sioux.* New York: Pocket Books, 1972.

Nerburn, Kent, and Louise Mengelkoch, eds. *Native American Wisdom.* San Rafael, Calif.: New World Library, 1991.

Niethammer, Carolyn. *Daughters of the Earth: The Lives and Legends of American Indian Women.* New York: Macmillan Publishing Company, 1977.

Oswalt, Wendell H. *This Land Was Theirs: A Study of North American Indians.* New York: John Wiley & Sons, 1978.

Owen, Roger C., et. al. *The North American Indians: A Sourcebook.* New York: Macmillan Publishing Company, 1967.

Oxendine, Joseph B. *American Indian Sports Heritage*. Champaign, Ill.: Human Kinetics Publishers, Inc., 1988.

Parker, Arthur C. *The History of the Seneca Indians*. New York: Ira J. Friedman, Inc., 1926.

————. *The Indian How Book*. New York: Dover Publications, Inc., 1975.

Peterson, Susan. *The Living Tradition of Maria Martinez: A Pueblo Ceramic Celebration*. Tokyo: Kodansha International, 1977.

Red Fox, Chief William. *The Memoirs of Chief Red Fox*. New York: McGraw-Hill, 1971.

Roe, Melvin W., ed. *Readings in the History of the American Indian*. New York: MSS Educational Publishing Company, Inc., 1971.

Rosen, Kenneth, ed. *The Man to Send Rain Clouds: Contemporary Stories by American Indians*. New York: Vintage Books, 1974.

Sacred Circles: Two Thousand Years of North American Art. London: Arts Council of Great Britain, 1977.

Schusky, Ernest. *The Right To Be Indian*. San Francisco: American Indian Educational Publishers, 1970.

Silverberg, Robert. *Mound Builders of Ancient America: The Archaeology of a Myth*. Greenwich, Conn.: New York Graphic Society, Ltd., 1968.

Sober, Nancy H. *The Intruders: The Illegal Residents of the Cherokee Nation, 1866–1907*. 2nd Ed. Tulsa, Okla.: Cherokee Books, 1991.

Sorkin, Alan L. *American Indians and Federal Aid*. Washington, D.C.: The Brookings Institution, 1971.

Spencer, Robert F., et. al. *The Native Americans: Ethnology and Backgrounds of the North American Indians*. New York: Harper & Row, 1977.

Steele, Ian K. *Betrayals: Fort William Henry and the "Massacre."* New York: Oxford University Press, 1990.

Stewart, Omer C. *Peyote Religion: A History*. Norman, Okla.: University of Oklahoma Press, 1987.

Stone, Eric. *Medicine Among the American Indians*. Philadelphia: Paul B. Hoeber, Inc., 1932.

Stoutenburgh, John, Jr. *Dictionary of the American Indian.* New York: Bonanza Books, 1960.

Sturtevant, William C., ed. *Handbook of North American Indians.* 20 vols. Washington, D.C.: Smithsonian Institution, 1978–1993.

Taylor, Graham D. *The New Deal and American Indian Tribalism: The Administration of the Indian Reorganization Act, 1934–1945.* Lincoln: University of Nebraska Press, 1980.

Terrell, John Upton. *Apache Chronicle.* New York: World Publishing, 1972.

Thornton, Russell. *American Indian Holocaust and Survival: A Population History Since 1492.* Norman, Okla.: The University of Oklahoma Press, 1990.

Tooker, Elisabeth, ed. *Native North American Spirituality of the Eastern Woodlands: Sacred Myths, Dreams, Visions, Speeches, Healing Formulas, Rituals and Ceremonies.* New York: Paulist Press, 1979.

Turner, Frederick W., ed. *The Portable North American Reader.* New York: Penguin Books, 1977.

Underhill, Ruth M. *The Navajos.* Norman, Okla.: The University of Oklahoma Press, 1967.

Utley, Robert M. *Frontier Regulars: The United States Army and the Indian, 1866–1891.* Lincoln, Nebr.: University of Nebraska Press, 1984.

―――. *Last Days of the Sioux Nation.* New Haven: Yale University Press, 1963.

Versluis, Arthur. *Sacred Earth: The Spiritual Landscape of Native America.* Rochester, N.Y.: Inner Traditions International, 1992.

Viola, Herman J. *Diplomats in Buckskins: A History of Indian Delegations in Washington City.* Washington, D.C.: Smithsonian, 1981.

Weatherford, Jack. *Indian Givers: How the Indians of the Americas Transformed the World.* New York: Fawcett, 1988.

―――. *Native Roots: How Indians Enriched America.* New York: Fawcett, 1991.

Weslager, C. A. *The Delaware Indians: A History.* New Brunswick, N.J.: Rutgers University Press, 1972.

White, Robert. *Tribal Assets: The Rebirth of Native America.* New York: Holt and Company, 1990.

White Deer of Autumn. *The Native American Book of Change.* Hillsboro, Oregon: Beyond Words Publishing, Inc. 1992.

———. *The Native American Book of Life.* Hillsboro, Oregon: Beyond Words Publishing, Inc., 1992.

———. *The Native American Book of Knowledge.* Hillsboro, Oregon: Beyond Words Publishing Inc., 1992.

Williams, Robert A., Jr. *The American Indian in Western Legal Thought: The Discourses of Conquest.* New York: Oxford University Press, 1990.

Wissler, Clark. *Indians of the United States.* Garden City, N.J.: Doubleday, 1966.

Woodward, Grace Steele. *Pocahontas.* Norman, Okla.: The University of Oklahoma Press, 1969.

Wright, J. Leitch, Jr. *The Only Land They Knew: The Tragic Story of the American Indians in the Old South.* New York: The Free Press, 1981.

INDEX

Adams, John, 70
Adams, John Quincy, 70, 76
Administration for Native Americans, 160-161
Africans, African-Americans, 59, 85, 102, 111
Algonkian, 27-28, 32-33, 44-47, 119
American Academy on Mental Retardation, 13
American Board of Commissioners for Foreign Missions, 134
American Indian Bible Institute, 139
American Indian Defense Association, 106-107, 109
American Indian Religious Freedom Act (1978), 111
Andrade, Ron, 15
Apaches, 13, 24-25, 30, 84, 89-91
Assemblies of God, 138-139
Athabascan, 24

Bahais, 137-138
Bahnimtewa, Stanley, 14
Bailey, Marsha, 115
Baptists, 80, 123-124
Bartlette, Don, 12-13
Bascom, George, 90
Battle of Grassy Grass, 95-97
Battle of Little Big Horn, 95-97
Battle of Rosebud, 95
Battle of Thames (1813), 74
Benevolent Empire, 133
Bible, 33, 59, 61-62, 114-115, 119, 122, 125, 128, 131, 133-134, 149-151
bison, 30-31, 49, 98
Black Elk, 98-99
Blackfoot, 12, 30
Black Hawk, 83
Blackhawk War (1832), 79
Black Hills, 48-50, 93-94
Black Horse, 16
Black Kettle, 92
Boarding School Movement, 99-105, 107

Brothertown, 127
Buffalo Bill's Wild West Show, 55
Bureau of Indian Affairs, 81-83, 95, 98, 100, 105, 107-110, 156
Bush, George W., 16, 86
Butler, Elihu, 113-114, 132
Butler, Richard, 66

Cabot, Sebastian, 58
Caddoan, 27
Cahokia, 26
Calhoun, John C., 71, 82, 133
California Gold Rush, 82-83
Campbell, Ben Nighthorse, 16-17
Carlisle Indian Industrial School, 100, 102-105, 112
Cayugas, 29, 45
Cheeshahteaumuck, Caleb, 120
Cherokee, 11, 27, 42, 58, 65, 75, 77-81, 84, 113-115, 132, 161

Cherokee Phoenix, 113

Cheyenne, 16-17, 84, 91-93, 95-96

Chickamauga, 65

Chickasaw, 27, 42, 75, 77-78

Chippewa, 12, 48

Chiricahua, 13

Choctaws, 26-27, 42, 77-78, 138-139

Christianity, 15, 18, 33, 59, 61-62, 79-80, 89, 97, 101-102, 104, 113-140, 147, 150-151, 160

Chungke, 44

"Civilization Fund," 70, 132-133

Civil War, 82-85, 89, 91-92, 99, 100, 115

Cochise, 89-90

Colby, Leonard Wright, 55-56

Colby, Marguerite Elizabeth, 55-56

Coles, Robert, 141

Collier, John, 106-110

Columbus, Christopher, 14, 21, 56, 158

Comanche, 148

Congregationalists, 113-115, 118-129, 134

Confederation Congress, 67

Constitution of the United States, 68-69, 78, 85

Cooper, Chauncey Miller Rose, 12

Cooper, John C., 11-12

Cornstalk, 65

Craig, Russell, 155-157, 159-160

Crazy Horse, 92, 95-97

Creek War, 75-76, 78

Creeks, 26, 42, 73, 75-78

Crook, George, 95

Crow, 96

Curtis Act (1898), 99

Curtis, Charles, 16, 108

Custer, George Armstrong, 91-98, 102

Dakota, 31

Douvan, Elizabeth, 141

Dover, Bill, 115

Dartmouth's "indian education program," 127

Dawes Act, 87-88, 106-107, 109, 111

Dawes Commission, 99, 103

Dawes, Henry L., 103

Declaration of Independence, 65

Dekanawida, 28-29

Delawares, 46-47, 58, 129-131

Diegueno, 15

Dragging Canoe, 65

Dutch West India Company, 60

Earl of Dartmouth, 127

Eastman, Charles Alexander (Ohiyesa), 149

Edwards, Jonathan, 128

Eliot, John, 33, 118-123

Erie, 29

Erikson, Erik, 141-146, 151

Europeans, 18, 21-23, 25-26, 28, 31-33, 36-37, 47-48, 50-51, 56-66, 72-74, 76, 79, 88, 101, 106, 115-119, 121-122, 126-129, 131, 139, 146-147, 149-151, 153, 157-158

Fetterman, William, 92

Five Civilized Nations, 12, 77, 84

Fort Marion, 100-101

Fort Pitt, 131

Fort Sill, 90-91, 100

Franciscans, 117

French and Indian War, 63-64, 128

Friends of the Indian, 102

Gadsden Purchase (1853), 82

Gatewood, Charles B., 91

General Allotment Act, 87-88, 99

George, Dan, 164

Geronimo, 13, 89-92

Ghost Dance Religion, 98, 140

Gnadenhutten, 130-131

"Golden Triangle," 59

Grant, Frederick, 93

Grant, Ulysses S., 85, 93-95

Great Awakening, 125, 128

Great New Moon Feast, 43

Great Spirit, 50, 52-53, 93, 98, 148

Great War for Empire, 63-64

Green Maize Feast, 43
Gutenberg, Johannes, 9

Hadjo, Masse, 140
Hampton Normal and
Agricultural School,
102
Handsome Lake, 47-48
Harrison, William
Henry, 73-74
Harvard "indian
college," 120
Hiacoomes, Joel, 120
Hiawatha, 28-29
Hill, Charlie, 158
Hilton, John, 35
Hitler, Adolf, 88
Hoover, Herbert, 16,
108
Hopewell, 25-26, 30
Hopi, 14, 24, 36, 38, 57
Housatonic Mahicans,
123, 127-129
Hunkpapa, 9, 94
Huron, 28-29, 57, 118
Huronia, 57

Ickes, Harold, 109-110
Indian Citizenship Act
(1924), 105
Indian Claims
Commission, 110
Indian Claims
Limitation Act
(1982), 110
"Indian Country," 50,
64, 66, 71, 81-83, 99,
115, 129-130
Indian Dialogues, 120-22
Indian Removal Act
(1830), 65, 77, 81
Indian Reorganization
Act (1934), 109

Indian Self-
Determination and
Education
Assistance Act
(1975), 111
Indian Wars, 71, 73, 81-
85
Intercourse Act of 1790,
68
Iroquoian, Iroquois, 27-
28, 44-45, 47, 57,
118, 124-125
Iroquois Confederacy,
29, 57-58

Jackson, Andrew, 71-72,
75-81, 114-115
Jamestown, 62-63
Jeffers, Anna, 12
Jefferson, Thomas, 33-
34, 48, 65, 70, 73, 75
Jesuits, 97, 117-118
Johnson Holy Rock, 13-
14
Johnson, Sir William,
63-64
Jones, Evan, 80
Joseph, Chief, 112

Kaw, 108
Kieft, Willem, 61
King Philip's War
(1675-1676), 122
Kiowa, 149

lacrosse, 44-45
La Jolla, 15
Lakota, 9, 13, 17, 31,
48-50, 92-95
League of Five Nations,
28-29, 45
Lee, George P., 137
Lewis and Clark

Expedition, 33-36,
48
Lewis, Meriwether, 33-
36, 48
Lichtenau, 131
Lindquist, Gustavus
E. E., 138
Little Big Horn, 16
longhouse, 45-46
Longhouse Religion,
47-48
Lost Bird, 55-56, 86
Lost Bird Society, 56
Louisiana Purchase and
Territory, 48, 69, 71
Luiseno, 15
Luther Standing Bear,
148, 162

McLaughlin, James, 98
Madison, James, 73
maize, 28, 42-43
Makah, 32, 39
Manypenny, George,
82-83
Marshall, John, 77-78,
114
Martha's Vineyard, 120
Massachusett, 33, 119-
120
Massachusetts Bay
Colony, 59, 61-62,
118-124, 127-129
Mather, Cotton, 134
Mather, Increase, 62
Mayflower, 59
Mayhew, Thomas, Jr.,
120
Mdewakanton, 31
Meriam Report (1928),
107-108
Methodists, 79, 132
Mexican War, 82

Miles, Nelson A., 91
Miller, Ouida, 13
Mills, Billy, 17
Mississippian, 26, 42
Mohawks, 28-29, 45, 57
Mohegans, 14-15, 125
Mohicans, 14
Monroe, James, 70-71, 133
Moor's Charity School, 125
Moravians, 131-132
Mormons, 137
Morse, Jedidiah, 71
Mound Builders, 25-26
Muskogean, 27

Nakota, 31
Natchez, 26
Natick, 122
National Association of Evangelicals, 10, 136
National Congress of American Indians, 15
National Council of Churches, 10
Native American Language Act (1990), 86
Native Americans, 21, 115, 120, 139-140, 164
  assimilation policy toward, 85-86, 88, 99-106, 110, 116-123 125-130, 132-139
  cultural regions, 22-33
  disease, 56-58, 105-106, 153
  disenfranchised, 85
  during Civil War, 82-85

during Early National Period, 68-81
during Revolutionary War, 65-66, 129-130
during twentieth century, 105-112, 135-139
extermination policy toward, 85, 87-88, 97-99, 130-132, 140, 150
indian rights activists, 99-102, 106-111, 113-115, 123-125, 132, 135, 140
languages, 22, 24, 27-28, 32-33, 86, 101, 103-104, 114, 116-117, 119-120, 123, 128, 134-135, 162
lifestyles, customs, and beliefs, 36-51, 97, 116-118, 120-126, 139, 146-151
modern role models, 10-18, 159, 163
prospects, 158-164
slavery, 58-60, 90
sports, 44-45, 147
toll of disruption on, 151-158
traditional life stages, 142-146
white attitudes toward, 11, 13-15, 18, 21-22, 25-26, 31, 47-48, 50-51, 55-56, 58-88, 90-140, 150, 153-161
women, 11, 13-15, 18, 37, 41, 43-46, 55-56,

58-59, 61, 80, 92, 96-97, 103, 125, 142, 144-145, 152, 154-157
worldview, 51-53, 94-95, 106, 116, 121, 146-151
Native American Church, 10, 136
"Native American Decade of Harvest," 138
Navajos, 24-25, 84, 110
Neutrals, 57
New Amsterdam, 60-61
New Enchota, 113
New Gnadenhutten, 131
New Stockbridge, 127, 129-130
Nez Pierce, 112
Nipissings, 57
Northwest Ordinance and Territory, 67-69, 73-74

Occom, Samson, 125-127
Oglala, 49, 95, 98-99, 148
Ohiyesa, 149
Olympic Games, 16-17
Oneidas, 29, 45, 126, 129, 158
Onondagas, 29, 45
Osage, 104
Osceola, 79
Ottawa, 138
"outing system," 104

Pan Am Games, 16
Papago, 23
Park Hill Mission, 115

Pendleton, George
  Hunt, 87-88
Penn, William, 124-125
Penobscot, 12
Pequot, 59
Pequot War, 119
Peter, Rev. Simon, 138-
  139
Peter, William Earl, 139
Peters, Mike, 138
Petun, 57
peyote, 136
physiognomy, pseudo-
  science of, 101
Pilgrims, 58
Pima, 23
Plymouth, 57
Pocahontas, 58
potlatch, 40
Poussaint, Alvin, 141
Powhatan, 57
powwow, 161
Pratt, Richard Henry,
  100-105, 112, 134-
  135
"praying indians,"
  "praying towns,"
  119-120, 122
Presbyterians, 126, 129,
  132, 134
Public Health Service,
  156-157, 161
Pueblos, 24, 36-39, 57,
  106, 116-117
Puritans, 47, 59, 61-62,
  118-129

Quakers, 108

rancherias, 23-24
Rausch, Marion June
  Palette, 5, 18
Real, Gasper Corte, 58

Red Cloud, 85
Red Jacket, 157-158
Red Sticks, 75-76
Religious Freedom
  Restoration Act, 10
Reservations, 25, 67,
  83-88, 94-95, 97-98,
  100, 102-109, 122,
  138, 153-157, 160-
  164
  Mescalero, 13, 90
  Pine Ridge, 91
  Rosebud, 91
  Standing Rock, 9-10,
  98
Revolutionary War, 64-
  66, 129-130
Rhoads, Charles, 108
Richardson, Edwin
  ("Strong-Legs"), 12,
  159
Roman Catholics, 97,
  116-118, 136
Roosevelt, Franklin
  Delano, 108-110
Roosevelt, Theodore,
  90-91
Ross, John, 79

Sac and Fox-
  Potawatomi, 17
Salem Witchcraft Trials,
  124
Sand Creek Massacre
  (1864), 84
Santee, 31, 149
Satanta (chief), 149
Scattergood, Henry, 108
Schlepp, Lydia
  Goodhouse, 5, 18
Schonbrunn, 131
Scott, Winfield, 79-80
Seattle (chief), 164

Seminoles, 27, 42, 77-
  79
Seminole Wars, 78-79
Senecas, 29, 45, 47-48,
  57, 157-158
Sequoya, 113
Sergeant, John, 127-128
Sergeant, John, Jr., 128-
  129
Seven Years' War, 63-64
Sewall, Samuel, 124
Shawnee, 65, 73-74
Sheridan, Philip H., 95,
  100
Sherman, William
  Tecumseh, 85
Shoshoni, 30
Siberia, 22
Siouan, 27
Sioux, 9, 11, 31, 48-50,
  55-56, 83-86, 88-89,
  91-99, 140-142,
  148-149
Sisseton, 31
Sitting Bull, 9-10, 91,
  94-98, 163
Smith, John, 59
Society for the
  Propagation of the
  Gospel in New
  England, 124, 128
Spotted Tail, 135
Squanto, 58-59
Standing Bull, 49
Stand Watie, 84
Stockbridge, 127-129
Sun Father, 38
Supreme Court, 10, 77-
  78, 105, 111, 113-
  115
Susquehannock, 29

Tantaquidgeon, Gladys,

14-15
Tecumseh, 73-75
Ten Bears, 148
Tenskwatawa, 73-74
Teton, 31, 48
Thorpe, Jim, 17
    tipis, 31, 50
"Trail of Tears," 11, 79-
    81, 115
Treaty of Fort Laramie
    (1851), 83
Treaty of Ghent (1815),
    74
Treaty of New Echota
    (1836), 79
Treaty of Paris (1783),
    66
Tuscarora, 29

Union of American
    Hebrew
    Congregations, 10
U.S. Government, 9-10,
    12, 15-17, 31, 33-34,
    48, 50, 65-86, 88-91,
    93-95, 99-100, 102-
    112, 114-115, 129-
    130, 132-133,

136-137, 140, 154,
    156-158, 160-161
"Utmost Good Faith"
    clause, 67-69
Verrazano, Giovanni da,
    58

Virgil, 126
vision quest, 52

Wahpekute, 31
Wahpeton, 31
Wakan Tanka, 50
Wampanoag, 58
War of 1812, 70, 72, 74-
    77, 79
Warren, Tom, 35
Washington, George,
    69-70, 130, 158
Wenro, 57
Westward Movement,
    21-22
Wheelock, Eleazar, 125-
    127
wigwams, 47
Wilbur, Ray Lyman, 108
Williams, Roger, 62,
    123-124

Williamson, David, 131
Winthrop, John, 61-62,
    124
Wool, John E., 79
Worcester, Samuel
    Austin, 113-115,
    132
World War I, 12, 105-
    106
World War II, 109-111
Wounded Knee
    Massacre, 55, 88-89,
    91, 98-99, 140
Wounded Knee
    Reoccupation
    (1973), 111

Yamparika, 148
Yankton, 11, 31
Yanktonai, 31
Yuma, 23-24
Yurok, 32, 39, 141-142

Zeisberger, David, 131-
    132
Zuni, 24, 36, 38